Storm Real-time Processing Cookbook

Efficiently process unbounded streams of data in real time

Quinton Anderson

[PACKT] open source
PUBLISHING
community experience distilled

BIRMINGHAM - MUMBAI

Storm Real-time Processing Cookbook

First published: August 2013

Production Reference: 1190813

Published by Packt Publishing Ltd.
Livery Place
35 Livery Street
Birmingham B3 2PB, UK.

ISBN 978-1-78216-442-5

www.packtpub.com

Cover Image by Suresh Mogre (suresh.mogre.99@gmail.com)

Credits

Author
Quinton Anderson

Reviewers
Maarten Ectors
Alexey Kachayev
Paco Nathan

Acquisition Editor
Usha Iyer

Lead Technical Editor
Madhuja Chaudhari

Technical Editors
Hardik B. Soni
Dennis John

Copy Editors
Mradula Hegde
Alfida Paiva
Laxmi Subramanian
Aditya Nair
Sayanee Mukherjee

Project Coordinator
Navu Dhillon

Proofreaders
Stephen Copestake
Clyde Jenkins

Indexer
Mariammal Chettiyar

Graphics
Abhinash Sahu

Production Coordinator
Prachali Bhiwandkar

Cover Work
Prachali Bhiwandkar

About the Author

Quinton Anderson is a software engineer with a background and focus on real-time computational systems. His career has been split between building real-time communication systems for defense systems and building enterprise applications within financial services and banking. Quinton does not align himself with any particular technology or programming language, but rather prefers to focus on sound engineering and polyglot development. He is passionate about open source, and is an active member of the Storm community; he has also enjoyed delivering various Storm-based solutions.

Quinton's next area of focus is machine learning; specifically, Deep Belief networks, as they pertain to robotics. Please follow his blog entries on Computational Theory, general IT concepts, and Deep Belief networks for more information.

You can find more information on Quinton via his LinkedIn profile (`http://au.linkedin.com/pub/quinton-anderson/37/422/11b/`) or more importantly, view and contribute to the source code available at his GitHub (`https://github.com/quintona`) and Bitbucket (`https://bitbucket.org/qanderson`) accounts.

I would like to thank the Storm community for their efforts in building a truly awesome platform for the open source community; a special mention, of course, to the core author of Storm, Nathan Marz.

I would like to thank my wife and children for putting up with my long working hours spent on this book and other related projects. Your effort in making up for my absence is greatly appreciated, and I love you all very dearly. I would also like to thank all those who participated in the review process of this book.

About the Reviewers

Maarten Ectors is an executive who is an expert in cloud computing, big data, and disruptive innovations. Maarten's strengths are his combination of deep technical and business skills as well as strategic insights.

Currently, Maarten is responsible for the cloud strategy at Canonical—the company behind Ubuntu—where he is changing the future of cloud, big data, and other disruptive innovations. Previously, Maarten had his own company and was defining and executing the cloud strategy of a global mobile company. Maarten worked for Nokia Siemens Networks in several roles. He was heading cloud and disruptive innovation, founded *Startups@NSN*, was responsible for implementing offshoring in Europe, and so on. Earlier, he worked as the Director of professional services for Telcordia (now Ericsson) and as a Senior Project / Product Manager for a dotcom. Maarten started his career at Accenture, where he was active in Java developments, portals, mobile applications, content management, ecommerce, security, project management, and so on.

I would like to thank my family for always being there for me. Especially my wonderful wife, Esther, and my great kids.

Alexey Kachayev began his development career in a small team creating an open source CMS for social networks. For over 2 years, he had been working as a Software Engineer at CloudMade, developing geo-relative technology for enterprise clients in Python and Scala. Currently, Alexey is the CTO at Attendify and is focused on development of a distributed applications platform in Erlang. He is an active speaker at conferences and an open source contributor (working on projects in Python, Clojure, and Haskell).

His area of professional interests include distributed systems and algorithms, types theory, and functional language compilers.

I would like to thank Nathan Marz and the Storm project contributors team for developing such a great technology and spreading great ideas.

Paco Nathan is the Chief Scientist at Mesosphere in San Francisco. He is a recognized expert in Hadoop, R, Data Science, and Cloud Computing, and has led innovative data teams building large-scale apps for the past decade. Paco is an evangelist for the Mesos and Cascading open source projects. He is also the author of *Enterprise Data Workflows with Cascading, O'Reilly*. He has a blog about Data Science at `http://liber118.com/pxn/`.

www.packtpub.com

Support files, eBooks, discount offers and more

You might want to visit www.packtpub.com for support files and downloads related to your book.

Did you know that Packt offers eBook versions of every book published, with PDF and ePub files available? You can upgrade to the eBook version at www.packtpub.com and as a print book customer, you are entitled to a discount on the eBook copy. Get in touch with us at service@packtpub.com for more details.

At www.packtpub.com, you can also read a collection of free technical articles, sign up for a range of free newsletters and receive exclusive discounts and offers on Packt books and eBooks.

http://PacktLib.packtpub.com

Do you need instant solutions to your IT questions? PacktLib is Packt's online digital book library. Here, you can access, read and search across Packt's entire library of books.

Why Subscribe?

- Fully searchable across every book published by Packt
- Copy and paste, print and bookmark content
- On demand and accessible via web browser

Free Access for Packt account holders

If you have an account with Packt at www.packtpub.com, you can use this to access PacktLib today and view nine entirely free books. Simply use your login credentials for immediate access.

Table of Contents

Preface

Open source has changed the software landscape in many fundamental ways. There are many arguments that can be made for and against using open source in any given situation, largely in terms of support, risk, and total cost of ownership. Open source is more popular in certain settings than others, such as research institutions versus large institutional financial service providers. Within the emerging areas of web service providers, content provision, and social networking, open source is dominating the landscape. This is true for many reasons, cost being a large one among them. These solutions that need to grow to "Web scale" have been classified as "Big Data" solutions, for want of a better term. These solutions serve millions of requests per second with extreme levels of availability, all the while providing customized experiences for customers across a wide range of services.

Designing systems at this scale requires us to think about problems differently, architect solutions differently, and learn where to accept complexity and where to avoid it. As an industry, we have come to grips with designing batch systems that scale. Large-scale computing clusters following MapReduce, Bulk Synchronous Parallel, and other computational paradigms are widely implemented and well understood. The surge of innovation has been driven and enabled by open source, leaving even the top software vendors struggling to integrate Hadoop into their technology stack, never mind trying to implement some level of competition to it.

Customers, however, have grown an insatiable desire for more. More data, more services, more value, more convenience, and they want it now and at lower cost. As the sheer volume of data increases, the demand for real-time response time increases too. The next phase of computational platforms has arrived, and it is focused on real time, at scale. It represents many unique challenges, and is both theoretically and practically challenging.

This cookbook will help you master a platform, the Storm processor. The Storm processor is an open source, real-time computational platform written by Nathan Marz at Backtype, a social analytics company. It was later purchased by Twitter and released as open source. It has since thrived in an ever-expanding open source community of users, contributors, and success stories within production sites. At the time of writing this preface, the project was enjoying more than 6,000 stars on GitHub, 3,000 Twitter followers, has been benchmarked at over a million transactions per second per node, and has almost 80 reference customers with production instances of Storm.

These are extremely impressive figures. Moreover, you will find by the end of this book that it is also extremely enjoyable to deliver systems based on Storm, using whichever language is congruent with your way of thinking and delivering solutions.

This book is designed to teach you Storm with a series of practical examples. These examples are grounded in real-world use cases, and introduce various concepts as the book unfolds. Furthermore, the book is designed to promote DevOps practice around the Storm technology, enabling the reader to develop Storm solutions and deliver them reliably into production, where they create value.

An introduction to the Storm processor

A common criticism of open source projects is their lack of documentation. Storm does not suffer from this particular issue; the documentation for the project is excellent, well-written, and well-supplemented by the vibrant user community. This cookbook does not seek to duplicate this documentation but rather supplement it, driven largely by examples with conceptual and theoretical discussion where required. It is highly recommended that the reader take the time to read the Storm introductory documentation before proceeding to *Chapter 1, Setting Up Your Development Environment*, specifically the following pages of the Storm wiki:

> ▶ `https://github.com/nathanmarz/storm/wiki/Rationale`

> ▶ `https://github.com/nathanmarz/storm/wiki/Concepts`

> ▶ `https://github.com/nathanmarz/storm/wiki/Understanding-the-parallelism-of-a-Storm-topology`

What this book covers

Chapter 1, Setting Up Your Development Environment, will demonstrate the process of setting up a local development environment for Storm; this includes all required tooling and suggested development workflows.

Chapter 2, Log Stream Processing, will lead the reader through the process of creating a log stream processing solution, complete with a base statistics dashboard and log-searching capability.

Chapter 3, Calculating Term Importance with Trident, will introduce the reader to Trident, a data-flow abstraction that works on top of Storm to enable highly productive enterprise data pipelines.

Chapter 4, Distributed Remote Procedure Calls, will teach the user how to implement distributed remote procedure calls.

Chapter 5, Polyglot Topology, will guide the reader to develop a Polyglot technology and add new technologies to the list of already supported technologies.

Chapter 6, Integrating Storm with Hadoop, will guide the user through the process of integrating Storm with Hadoop, thus creating a complete Lambda architecture.

Chapter 7, Real-time Machine Learning, will provide the reader with a very basic introduction to machine learning as a topic, and provides various approaches to implementing it in real-time projects based on Storm.

Chapter 8, Continuous Delivery, will demonstrate how to set up a Continuous Delivery pipeline and deliver a Storm cluster reliably into an environment.

Chapter 9, Storm on AWS, will guide the user through various approaches to automated provisioning of a Storm cluster into the Amazon Computing Cloud.

What you need for this book

This book assumes a base environment of Ubuntu or Debian. The first chapter will guide the reader through the process of setting up the remaining required tooling. If the reader does not use Ubuntu as a developer operating system, any *Nix-based system is preferred, as all the recipes assume the existence of a bash command interface.

Who this book is for

Storm Real-time Processing Cookbook is ideal for developers who would like to learn real-time processing or would like to learn how to use Storm for real-time processing. It's assumed that you are a Java developer. Clojure, C++, and Ruby experience would be useful but is not essential. It would also be useful to have some experience with Hadoop or similar technologies.

Conventions

In this book, you will find a number of styles of text that distinguish between different kinds of information. Here are some examples of these styles, and an explanation of their meaning.

Code words in text, database table names, folder names, filenames, file extensions, pathnames, dummy URLs, user input, and Twitter handles are shown as follows: "You must then create your first spout by creating a new class named `HelloWorldSpout`, which extends from `BaseRichSpout` and is located in the `storm.cookbook` package."

A block of code is set as follows:

```xml
<repositories>

    <repository>
      <id>github-releases</id>
      <url>http://oss.sonatype.org/content/repositories
        /github-releases/</url>
    </repository>

    <repository>
      <id>clojars.org</id>
      <url>http://clojars.org/repo</url>
    </repository>

    <repository>
      <id>twitter4j</id>
      <url>http://twitter4j.org/maven2</url>
    </repository>
</repositories>
```

Any command-line input or output is written as follows:

```
mkdir FirstGitProject
cd FirstGitProject
git init
```

New terms and **important words** are shown in bold. Words that you see on the screen, in menus or dialog boxes for example, appear in the text like this: "Uncheck the **Use default location** checkbox."

 Warnings or important notes appear in a box like this.

 Tips and tricks appear like this.

Reader feedback

Feedback from our readers is always welcome. Let us know what you think about this book—what you liked or may have disliked. Reader feedback is important for us to develop titles that you really get the most out of.

To send us general feedback, simply send an e-mail to feedback@packtpub.com, and mention the book title via the subject of your message.

If there is a topic that you have expertise in and you are interested in either writing or contributing to a book, see our author guide on www.packtpub.com/authors.

Customer support

Now that you are the proud owner of a Packt book, we have a number of things to help you to get the most from your purchase.

Downloading the example code

You can download the example code files for all Packt books you have purchased from your account at http://www.packtpub.com. If you purchased this book elsewhere, you can visit http://www.packtpub.com/support and register to have the files e-mailed directly to you.

Open source versions of the code are maintained by the author at his Bitbucket account: https://bitbucket.org/qanderson.

Errata

Although we have taken every care to ensure the accuracy of our content, mistakes do happen. If you find a mistake in one of our books—maybe a mistake in the text or the code—we would be grateful if you would report this to us. By doing so, you can save other readers from frustration and help us improve subsequent versions of this book. If you find any errata, please report them by visiting http://www.packtpub.com/submit-errata, selecting your book, clicking on the **errata submission form** link, and entering the details of your errata. Once your errata are verified, your submission will be accepted and the errata will be uploaded on our website, or added to any list of existing errata, under the Errata section of that title. Any existing errata can be viewed by selecting your title from http://www.packtpub.com/support.

Piracy

Piracy of copyright material on the Internet is an ongoing problem across all media. At Packt, we take the protection of our copyright and licenses very seriously. If you come across any illegal copies of our works, in any form, on the Internet, please provide us with the location address or website name immediately so that we can pursue a remedy.

Please contact us at `copyright@packtpub.com` with a link to the suspected pirated material.

We appreciate your help in protecting our authors, and our ability to bring you valuable content.

Questions

You can contact us at `questions@packtpub.com` if you are having a problem with any aspect of the book, and we will do our best to address it.

1
Setting Up Your Development Environment

In this chapter we will cover:

- ▸ Setting up your development environment
- ▸ Distributed version control
- ▸ Creating a "Hello World" topology
- ▸ Creating a Storm cluster – provisioning the machines
- ▸ Creating a Storm cluster – provisioning Storm
- ▸ Deriving basic click statistics
- ▸ Unit testing a bolt
- ▸ Implementing an integration test
- ▸ Deploying to the cluster

Introduction

This chapter provides a very basic and practical introduction to the **Storm processor**. This will cover everything, from setting up your development environment to basic operational concerns in deploying your topologies and basic quality practices such as unit and integration testing of your Storm topology. Upon completion of this chapter, you will be able to build, test, and deliver basic Storm topologies.

This book does not provide a theoretical introduction to the Storm processor and its primitives and architecture. The author assumes that the readers have orientated themselves through online resources such as the Storm wiki.

 Delivery of systems is only achieved once a system is delivering a business value in a production environment consistently and reliably. In order to achieve this, quality and operational concerns must always be taken into account while developing your Storm topologies.

Setting up your development environment

A development environment consists of all the tools and systems that are required in order to start building Storm topologies. The focus of this book is on individual delivery of Storm with a focus on the technology; however, it must be noted that the development environment for a software development team, be it centralized or distributed, would require much more tooling and processes to be effective and is considered outside the scope of this book.

The following classes of tools and processes are required in order to effectively set up the development environment, not only from an on-going perspective, but also in terms of implementing the recipes in this book:

- SDK(s)
- Version control
- Build environment
- System provisioning tooling
- Cluster provisioning tooling

The provisioning and installation recipes in this book are based on Ubuntu; they are, however, quite portable to other Linux distributions. If you have any issues working with another distribution using these instructions, please seek support from the Storm mailing list at `https://groups.google.com/forum/#!forum/storm-user`.

 Environmental variables are the enemy of maintainable and available systems. Developing on one environment type and deploying on another is a very risky example of such a variable. Developing on your target type should be done whenever possible.

How to do it...

1. Download the latest J2SE 6 SDK from Oracle's website (`http://www.oracle.com/technetwork/java/javase/downloads/index.html`) and install it as follows:

    ```
    chmod 775 jdk-6u35-linux-x64.bin
    ```

```
yes | jdk-6u35-linux-x64.bin
mv jdk1.6.0_35 /opt
ln -s /opt/jdk1.6.0_35/bin/java /usr/bin
ln -s /opt/jdk1.6.0_35/bin/javac /usr/bin
JAVA_HOME=/opt/jdk1.6.0_35
export JAVA_HOME
PATH=$PATH:$JAVA_HOME/bin
export PATH
```

2. The version control system, Git, must then be installed:

```
sudo apt-get install git
```

3. The installation should then be followed by Maven, the build system:

```
sudo apt-get install mvn
```

4. Puppet, Vagrant, and VirtualBox must then be installed in order to provide application and environment provisioning:

```
sudo apt-get install virtualbox puppet vagrant
```

5. Finally, you need to install an IDE:

```
sudo apt-get install eclipse
```

 There is currently a debate around which fork of the Java SDK is to be used since Sun was acquired by Oracle. While the author understood the need for OpenJDK, the recipes in this book have been tested using the Oracle JDK. In general, there is no difference between OpenJDK and Oracle JDK, apart from the Oracle JDK being more stable but lagging behind in terms of features.

How it works...

The JDK is obviously required for any Java development to take place. GIT is an open source distributed version control system that has received wide adoption in recent years. A brief introduction to GIT will be presented shortly.

Maven is a widely used build system that prefers convention over configuration. Maven includes many useful features including the **Project Object Model** (**POM**), which allows us to manage our libraries, dependencies, and versions in an effective manner. Maven is backed by many binary repositories on the Internet that allow us to transparently maintain binary dependencies correctly and package our topologies for deployment.

Within the growing arena of **DevOps** and **Continuous Delivery**, the Puppet system is widely used to provide declarative server provisioning of Linux and other operating systems and applications. Puppet provides us with the ability to *program* the state of our servers and deployment environments. This is important because our server's state can then be maintained within a version control system such as GIT and manual changes to servers can be safely removed. This provides many advantages, including deterministic **Mean Time to Recovery** (**MTTR**) and audit trail, which, in general, means making systems more stable. This is also an important step on the path towards continuous delivery.

Vagrant is a very useful tool within development environments. It allows the automation of provisioning of VirtualBox virtual machines. Within the context of the Storm processor, this is important, given that it is a cluster-based technology. In order to test a cluster, you must either build an actual cluster of machines or provision many virtual machines. Vagrant allows us to do this locally in a deterministic and declarative way.

A virtual machine is an extremely useful abstraction within the IT infrastructure, operations, and development. However, it must be noted that, while reduced performance is expected and acceptable within locally hosted VMs, their usability at all times depends entirely on the availability of RAM. The processing power is not a key concern, especially with most modern processors being extremely underutilized, although this is not necessarily the case once your topologies are working; it is recommended that you ensure your computer has at least 8 GB of RAM.

Distributed version control

Traditional version control systems are centralized. Each client contains a checkout of the files at their current version, depending on what branch the client is using. All previous versions are stored on the server. This has worked well, in such a way that it allows teams to collaborate closely and know to some degree what other members of the team are doing.

Centralized servers have some distinct downfalls that have led to the rise of distributed control systems. Firstly, the centralized server represents a single point of failure; if the server goes down or becomes unavailable for any reason, it becomes difficult for developers to work using their existing workflows. Secondly, if the data on the server is corrupt or lost for any reason, the history of the code base is lost.

Open source projects have been a large driver of distributed version controls, for both reasons, but mostly because of the collaboration models that distribution enables. Developers can follow a disciplined set of workflows on their local environments and then distribute these changes to one or many remote repositories when it is convenient to do so, in both a flat and hierarchical manner.

The obvious additional advantage is that there naturally exist many backups of the repository because each client has a complete mirror of the repository; therefore, if any client or server dies, it can simply be replicated back, once it has been restored.

How to do it...

Git is used in this book as the distributed version control system. In order to create a repository, you need to either clone or initialize a repository. For a new project that you create, the repository should be initialized.

1. First, let's create our project directory, as follows:

    ```
    mkdir FirstGitProject
    cd FirstGitProject
    git init
    ```

2. In order to test if the workflow is working, we need some files in our repository.

    ```
    touch README.txt
    vim README.txt
    ```

    Using `vim`, or any other text editor, simply add some descriptive text and press the *Insert* key. Once you have finished typing, simply hit the *Esc* key and then a colon, followed by `wq`; hit the *Enter* key.

3. Before you commit, review the status of the repository.

    ```
    git status
    ```

    This should give you an output that looks similar to the following:

    ```
    # On branch master
    # Initial commit
    # Untracked files:
    #       README.txt
    ```

4. Git requires that you add all files and folders manually; you can do it as follows:

    ```
    git add README.txt
    ```

5. Then commit the file using the following:

    ```
    git commit -a
    ```

6. This will open a `vim` editor and allow you to add your comments.

 You can specify the commit message directly while issuing the command, using the −m flag.

Without pushing this repository to a remote host, you will essentially be placing it under the same risk as that of a centralized host. It is therefore important to push the repository to a remote host. Both www.github.com and www.bitbucket.org are good options for free-hosted Git services, providing that you aren't pushing your corporate intellectual property there for public consumption. This book uses bitbucket.org. In order to push your repository to this remote host, simply navigate there in your browser and sign up for an account.

Once the registration process is complete, create a new repository using the menu system.

Enter the following values in order to create the repository:

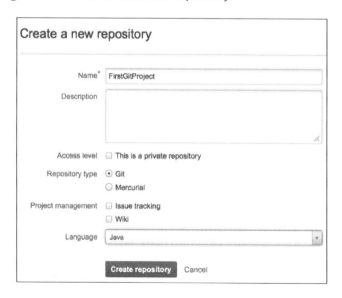

Once the repository is created, you need to add the remote repository to your local repository and push the changes to the remote repository.

```
git remote add origin https://[user]@bitbucket.org/[user]/
firstgitproject.git
```

```
git push origin master
```

You must replace [user] in the preceding command with your registered username.

 Cloning of a repository will be covered in later recipes, as will some standard version control workflows.

Creating a "Hello World" topology

The "Hello World" topology, as with all "Hello World" applications, is of no real use to anyone, except to illustrate some really basic concepts. The "Hello World" topology will show how to create a Storm project including a simple spout and bolt, build it, and execute it in the local cluster mode.

How to do it...

1. Create a new project folder and initialize your Git repository.

   ```
   mkdir HelloWorld
   cd HelloWorld
   git init
   ```

2. We must then create the Maven project file as follows:

   ```
   vim pom.xml
   ```

3. Using vim, or any other text editor, you need to create the basic XML tags and project metadata for the "Hello World" project.

   ```xml
   <project xmlns="http://maven.apache.org/POM/4.0.0"
   xmlns:xsi="http://www.w3.org/2001/XMLSchema-instance"
     xsi:schemaLocation="http://maven.apache.org/POM/4.0.0
     http://maven.apache.org/xsd/maven-4.0.0.xsd">

     <modelVersion>4.0.0</modelVersion>

     <groupId>storm.cookbook</groupId>
     <artifactId>hello-world</artifactId>
   ```

```
<version>0.0.1-SNAPSHOT</version>
<packaging>jar</packaging>

<name>hello-world</name>
<url>https://bitbucket.org/[user]/hello-world</url>

<properties>
    <project.build.sourceEncoding>UTF-8</project.build.
sourceEncoding>
</properties>

</project>
```

4. We then need to declare which Maven repositories we need to fetch our dependencies from. Add the following to the pom.xml file within the project tags:

```
<repositories>

    <repository>
      <id>github-releases</id>
      <url>http://oss.sonatype.org/content/repositories
        /github-releases/</url>
    </repository>

    <repository>
      <id>clojars.org</id>
      <url>http://clojars.org/repo</url>
    </repository>

    <repository>
      <id>twitter4j</id>
      <url>http://twitter4j.org/maven2</url>
    </repository>
</repositories>
```

> You can override these repositories using your .m2 and settings.xml files, the details of which are outside the scope of this book; however, this is extremely useful within development teams where dependency management is the key.

5. We then need to declare our dependencies by adding them within the project tags:

```
<dependencies>
    <dependency>
      <groupId>junit</groupId>
      <artifactId>junit</artifactId>
```

```
      <version>3.8.1</version>
      <scope>test</scope>
    </dependency>

    <dependency>
      <groupId>storm</groupId>
      <artifactId>storm</artifactId>
      <version>0.8.1</version>
      <!-- keep storm out of the jar-with-dependencies -->
      <scope>provided</scope>
    </dependency>

    <dependency>
      <groupId>com.googlecode.json-simple</groupId>
      <artifactId>json-simple</artifactId>
      <version>1.1</version>
    </dependency>

  </dependencies>
```

6. Finally we need to add the `build` plugin definitions for Maven:

```
<build>
  <plugins>
    <!--
    bind the maven-assembly-plugin to the package phase
    this will create a jar file without the Storm
    dependencies suitable for deployment to a cluster.
      -->
    <plugin>
      <artifactId>maven-assembly-plugin</artifactId>
      <configuration>
        <descriptorRefs>
          <descriptorRef>jar-with-dependencies</descriptorRef>
        </descriptorRefs>
        <archive>
          <manifest>
            <mainClass></mainClass>
          </manifest>
        </archive>
      </configuration>
      <executions>
        <execution>
          <id>make-assembly</id>
          <phase>package</phase>
          <goals>
            <goal>single</goal>
          </goals>
        </execution>
      </executions>
    </plugin>
```

```
        <plugin>
          <groupId>com.theoryinpractise</groupId>
          <artifactId>clojure-maven-plugin</artifactId>
          <version>1.3.8</version>
          <extensions>true</extensions>
          <configuration>
           <sourceDirectories>
            <sourceDirectory>src/clj</sourceDirectory>
           </sourceDirectories>
          </configuration>
          <executions>
          <execution>
              <id>compile</id>
              <phase>compile</phase>
              <goals>
                  <goal>compile</goal>
              </goals>
            </execution>
              <execution>
              <id>test</id>
              <phase>test</phase>
              <goals>
                  <goal>test</goal>
              </goals>
            </execution>
          </executions>

        </plugin>
        <plugin>
          <groupId>org.apache.maven.plugins</groupId>
          <artifactId>maven-compiler-plugin</artifactId>
          <configuration>
            <source>1.6</source>
            <target>1.6</target>
          </configuration>
        </plugin>
      </plugins>
    </build>
```

7. With the POM file complete, save it using the *Esc* + : + wq + *Enter* key sequence and complete the required folder structure for the Maven project:

```
mkdir src
cd src
mkdir test
mkdir main
cd main
mkdir java
```

8. Then return to the project root folder and generate the Eclipse project files using the following:

```
mvn eclipse:eclipse
```

 The Eclipse project files are a generated artifact, much as a `.class` file, and should not be included in your Git checkins, especially since they contain client-machine-specific paths.

9. You must now start your Eclipse environment and import the generated project files into the workspace:

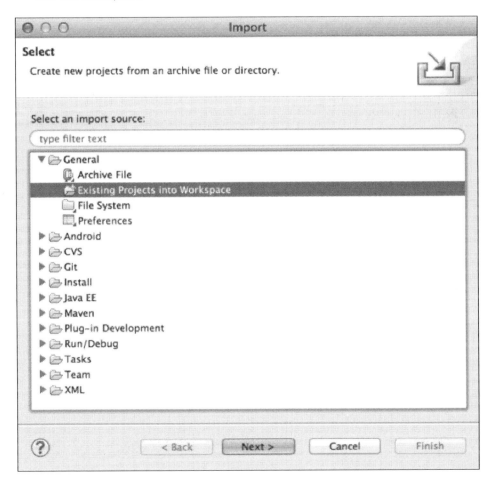

10. You must then create your first spout by creating a new class named
    `HelloWorldSpout`, which extends from `BaseRichSpout` and is located
    in the `storm.cookbook` package. Eclipse will generate a default spouts
    method for you. The spout will simply generate tuples based on random
    probability. Create the following member variables and construct the object:

    ```
    private SpoutOutputCollector collector;
      private int referenceRandom;
      private static final int MAX_RANDOM = 10;
      public HelloWorldSpout(){
        final Random rand = new Random();
        referenceRandom = rand.nextInt(MAX_RANDOM);
      }
    ```

11. After construction, the Storm cluster will open the spout; provide the following
    implementation for the `open` method:

    ```
    public void open(Map conf, TopologyContext context,
          SpoutOutputCollector collector) {
        this.collector = collector;
      }
    ```

12. The Storm cluster will repeatedly call the `nextTuple` method, which will do all the
    work of the spout. Provide the following implementation for the method:

    ```
    Utils.sleep(100);
        final Random rand = new Random();
        int instanceRandom = rand.nextInt(MAX_RANDOM);
        if(instanceRandom == referenceRandom){
          collector.emit(new Values("Hello World"));
        } else {
          collector.emit(new Values("Other Random Word"));
        }
    ```

13. Finally, you need to tell the Storm cluster which fields this spout emits within the
    `declareOutputFields` method:

    ```
    declarer.declare(new Fields("sentence"));
    ```

14. Once you have resolved all the required imports for the class, you need to create
    `HelloWorldBolt`. This class will consume the produced tuples and implement the
    required counting logic. Create the new class within the `storm.cookbook` package;
    it should extend the `BaseRichBolt` class. Declare a private member variable and
    provide the following implementation for the `execute` method, which does the work
    for this bolt:

```
String test = input.getStringByField("sentence");
    if("Hello World".equals(test)){
      myCount++;
      System.out.println("Found a Hello World! My Count is now: "
                         + Integer.toString(myCount));
    }
```

15. Finally, you need to bring the elements together and declare the Storm topology. Create a main class named `HelloWorldTopology` within the same package and provide the following main implementation:

```
TopologyBuilder builder = new TopologyBuilder();

        builder.setSpout("randomHelloWorld", new
                    HelloWorldSpout(), 10);
        builder.setBolt("HelloWorldBolt", new
                    HelloWorldBolt(), 2)
          .shuffleGrouping("randomHelloWorld");

        Config conf = new Config();
        conf.setDebug(true);

        if(args!=null && args.length > 0) {
            conf.setNumWorkers(3);

            StormSubmitter.submitTopology(args[0], conf,
              builder.createTopology());
        } else {

            LocalCluster cluster = new LocalCluster();
            cluster.submitTopology("test", conf,
                            builder.createTopology());
            Utils.sleep(10000);
            cluster.killTopology("test");
            cluster.shutdown();
        }
```

This will essentially set up the topology and submit it to either a local or remote Storm cluster, depending on the arguments passed to the `main` method.

16. After you have resolved the compiler issues, you can execute the cluster by issuing the following command from the project's root folder:

```
mvn compile exec:java -Dexec.classpathScope=compile -Dexec.
mainClass=storm.cookbook.HelloWorldTopology
```

How it works...

The following diagram describes the "Hello World" topology:

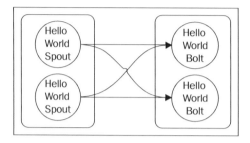

The spout essentially emits a stream containing one of the following two sentences:

▶   `Other Random Word`

▶   `Hello World`

Based on random probability, it works by generating a random number upon construction and then generates subsequent random numbers to test against the original member's variable value. When it matches, `Hello World` is emitted; during the remaining executions, the other random words are emitted.

The bolt simply matches and counts the instances of `Hello World`. In the current implementation, you will notice sequential increments being printed from the bolt. In order to scale this bolt, you simply need to increase the parallelism hint for the topology by updating the following line:

```
builder.setBolt("HelloWorldBolt", new HelloWorldBolt(), 3)
            .shuffleGrouping("randomHelloWorld");
```

The key parameter here is `parallism_hint`, which you can adjust upwards. If you execute the cluster again, you will then notice three separate counts that are printed independently and interweaved with each other.

You can scale a cluster after deployment by updating these hints using the Storm GUI or CLI; however, you can't change the topology structure without recompiling and redeploying the JAR. For the command-line option, please see the CLI documentation on the wiki available at the following link:

`https://github.com/nathanmarz/storm/wiki/`
`Command-line-client`

It is important to ensure that your project dependencies are declared correctly within your POM. The Storm JARs must be declared with the provided scope; if not, they would be packaged into your JAR; this would result in duplicate class files on the classpath within a deployed node of the cluster. Note that Storm checks for this classpath duplication; it will fail to start if you have included Storm into your distribution.

Downloading the example code

You can download the example code files for all Packt books you have purchased from your account at `http://www.packtpub.com`. If you purchased this book elsewhere, you can visit `http://www.packtpub.com/support` and register to have the files e-mailed directly to you.

Open source versions of the code are maintained by the author at his Bitbucket account at `https://bitbucket.org/qanderson`.

Creating a Storm cluster – provisioning the machines

Testing the cluster in the local mode is useful for debugging and verifying the basic functional logic of the cluster. It doesn't, however, give you a realistic view as to the operation of the cluster. Moreover, any development effort is only complete once the system is running in a production environment. This is a key consideration for any developer and is the cornerstone of the entire DevOps movement; regardless of the methodology, however, you must be able to reliably deploy your code into an environment. This recipe demonstrates how to create and provision an entire cluster directly from version control. There are many key principles in doing this:

▸ The state of any given server must be known at all times. It isn't acceptable that people can log into a server and make changes to its settings or files without strict version control being in place.

▸ Servers should be fundamentally immutable, with the state in some kind of separate volume. This allows deterministic recovery times of a server.

▸ If something causes problems in the delivery process, do it more often. In software development and IT operations, this applies heavily to disaster recovery and integration. Both tasks can only be performed often if they are automated.

▸ This book assumes that your destination production environment is a cluster (based on Amazon Web Services (AWS) EC2), which enables automatic scaling. Elastic auto-scaling is only possible where provisioning is automated.

The deployment of Storm topologies to an AWS cluster is the subject for a later chapter; however, the fundamentals will be presented in this recipe in a development environment.

How to do it...

Let's start by creating a new project as follows:

1. Create a new project named `vagrant-storm-cluster` with the following data structure:

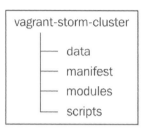

```
vagrant-storm-cluster
    ├── data
    ├── manifest
    ├── modules
    └── scripts
```

2. Using your favorite editor, create a file in the project root called `Vagrantfile`. Inside the file, you must create the file header and the configuration for the virtual machines that we want to create. We need at least one `nimbus` node, two `supervisor` nodes, and a `zookeeper` node:

```ruby
# -*- mode: ruby -*-
# vi: set ft=ruby :
boxes = [
    { :name => :nimbus, :ip => '192.168.33.100', :cpus =>2, :memory
        => 512 },
    { :name => :supervisor1, :ip => '192.168.33.101', :cpus
        =>4, :memory => 1024 },
    { :name => :supervisor2, :ip => '192.168.33.102', :cpus
        =>4, :memory => 1024 },
    { :name => :zookeeper1, :ip => '192.168.33.201', :cpus
        =>1, :memory => 512 }
]
```

> Note that the use of a single `zookeeper` node is only for development environments, as this cluster is not highly available. The purpose of this cluster is to test your topology logic in a realistic setting and identify stability issues.

3. You must then create the virtual machine provisioning for each machine, specialized by the previous configuration at execution time. The first set of properties defines the hardware, networking, and operating system:

```ruby
boxes.each do |opts|
    config.vm.define opts[:name] do |config|
        config.vm.box = "ubuntu12"
        config.vm.box_url =
```

```
              "http://dl.dropbox.com/u/1537815/precise64.box"
              config.vm.network :hostonly, opts[:ip]
        config.vm.host_name = "storm.%s" % opts[:name].to_s
        config.vm.share_folder "v-data", "/vagrant_data",
                            "./data", :transient => false
        config.vm.customize ["modifyvm", :id, "--memory",
                        opts[:memory]]
        config.vm.customize ["modifyvm", :id, "--cpus",
                        opts[:cpus] ] if opts[:cpus]
```

4. The provisioning of the application is then configured using a combination of the bash and Puppet scripts:

```
config.vm.provision :shell, :inline => "cp -fv /vagrant_data/hosts
/etc/hosts"

    config.vm.provision :shell, :inline => "apt-get update"
      # Check if the jdk has been provided
      if File.exist?("./data/jdk-6u35-linux-x64.bin") then
      config.vm.provision :puppet do |puppet|
        puppet.manifests_path = "manifests"
        puppet.manifest_file = "jdk.pp"
       end
      end

      config.vm.provision :puppet do |puppet|
      puppet.manifests_path = "manifests"
      puppet.manifest_file = "provisioningInit.pp"
      end

      # Ask puppet to do the provisioning now.
      config.vm.provision :shell, :inline => "puppet apply
      /tmp/storm-puppet/manifests/site.pp --verbose --
      modulepath=/tmp/storm-puppet/modules/ --debug"

    end
  end
end
```

The Vagrant file simply defines the hypervisor-level configuration and provisioning; the remaining provisioning is done through Puppet and is defined at two levels. The first level makes the base Ubuntu installation ready for application provisioning. The second level contains the actual application provisioning. In order to create the first level of provisioning, you need to create the JDK provisioning bash script and the provisioning initialization Puppet script.

5. In the `scripts` folder of the project, create the `installJdk.sh` file and populate it with the following code:

```
#!/bin/sh
echo "Installing JDK!"
chmod 775 /vagrant_data/jdk-6u35-linux-x64.bin
cd /root
yes | /vagrant_data/jdk-6u35-linux-x64.bin
/bin/mv /root/jdk1.6.0_35 /opt
/bin/rm -rv /usr/bin/java
/bin/rm -rv /usr/bin/javac
/bin/ln -s /opt/jdk1.6.0_35/bin/java /usr/bin
/bin/ln -s /opt/jdk1.6.0_35/bin/javac /usr/bin
JAVA_HOME=/opt/jdk1.6.0_35
export JAVA_HOME
PATH=$PATH:$JAVA_HOME/bin
export PATH
```

This will simply be invoked by the Puppet script in a declarative manner.

6. In the `manifest` folder create a file called `jdk.pp`:

```
$JDK_VERSION = "1.6.0_35"
package {"openjdk":
  ensure  =>  absent,
}
exec { "installJdk":
  command => "installJdk.sh",
    path => "/vagrant/scripts",
    logoutput => true,
    creates => "/opt/jdk${JDK_VERSION}",
}
```

7. In the `manifest` folder, create the `provisioningInit.pp` file and define the required packages and static variable values:

```
$CLONE_URL = "https://bitbucket.org/qanderson/storm-puppet.git"
$CHECKOUT_DIR="/tmp/storm-puppet"

package {git:ensure=> [latest,installed] }
package {puppet:ensure=> [latest,installed] }
package {ruby:ensure=> [latest,installed] }
package {rubygems:ensure=> [latest,installed] }
package {unzip:ensure=> [latest,installed] }

exec { "install_hiera":
  command => "gem install hiera hiera-puppet",
    path => "/usr/bin",
    require => Package['rubygems'],
}
```

For more information on **Hiera**, please see the Puppet documentation page at `http://docs.puppetlabs.com/hiera/1/index.html`.

8. You must then clone the repository, which contains the second level of provisioning:

```
exec { "clone_storm-puppet":
  command => "git clone ${CLONE_URL}",
  cwd => "/tmp",
    path => "/usr/bin",
    creates => "${CHECKOUT_DIR}",
    require => Package['git'],
}
```

9. You must now configure a Puppet plugin called Hiera, which is used to externalize properties from the provisioning scripts in a hierarchical manner:

```
exec {"/bin/ln -s /var/lib/gems/1.8/gems/hiera-puppet-1.0.0/ /tmp/
storm-puppet/modules/hiera-puppet":
  creates => "/tmp/storm-puppet/modules/hiera-puppet",
  require => [Exec['clone_storm-
              puppet'],Exec['install_hiera']]
}


#install hiera and the storm configuration
file { "/etc/puppet/hiera.yaml":
    source => "/vagrant_data/hiera.yaml",
    replace => true,
    require => Package['puppet']
}

file { "/etc/puppet/hieradata":
  ensure => directory,
  require => Package['puppet']
}

file {"/etc/puppet/hieradata/storm.yaml":
  source => "${CHECKOUT_DIR}/modules/storm.yaml",
    replace => true,
    require => [Exec['clone_storm-puppet'],File['/etc/puppet/
              hieradata']]
}
```

10. Finally, you need to populate the `data` folder. Create the Hiera base configuration file, `hiera.yaml`:

```
---
:hierarchy:
    - %{operatingsystem}
    - storm
:backends:
    - yaml
:yaml:
    :datadir: '/etc/puppet/hieradata'
```

11. The final datafile required is the host's file, which act as the DNS in our local cluster:

```
127.0.0.1         localhost
192.168.33.100    storm.nimbus
192.168.33.101    storm.supervisor1
192.168.33.102    storm.supervisor2
192.168.33.103    storm.supervisor3
192.168.33.104    storm.supervisor4
192.168.33.105    storm.supervisor5
192.168.33.201    storm.zookeeper1
192.168.33.202    storm.zookeeper2
192.168.33.203    storm.zookeeper3
192.168.33.204    storm.zookeeper4
```

 The host's file is not required in properly configured environments; however, it works nicely in our local "host only" development network.

The project is now complete, in that it will provision the correct virtual machines and install the base required packages; however, we need to create the Application layer provisioning, which is contained in a separate repository.

12. Initialize your Git repository for this project and push it to `bitbucket.org`.

How it works...

Provisioning is performed on three distinct layers:

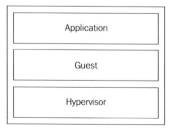

This recipe only works in the bottom two layers, with the Application layer presented in the next recipe. A key reason for the separation is that you will typically create different provisioning at these layers depending on the Hypervisor you are using for deployment. Once the VMs are provisioned, however, the application stack provisioning should be consistent through all your environments. This is key, in that it allows us to test our deployments hundreds of times before we get to production, and ensure that they are in a repeatable and version-controlled state.

In the development environment, VirtualBox is the Hypervisor with Vagrant and Puppet providing the provisioning. Vagrant works by specializing a base image of a VirtualBox. This base image represents a version-controlled artifact. For each box defined in our Vagrant file, the following parameters are specified:

- ▸ The base box
- ▸ The network settings
- ▸ Shared folders
- ▸ Memory and CPU settings for the VM

 This base provisioning does not include any of the baseline controls you would expect in a production environment, such as security, access controls, housekeeping, and monitoring. You must provision these before proceeding beyond your development environment. You can find these kinds of recipes on Puppet Forge (http://forge.puppetlabs.com/).

Provisioning agents are then invoked to perform the remaining heavy lifting:

```
config.vm.provision :shell, :inline => "cp -fv /vagrant_data/hosts /etc/
hosts"
```

The preceding command installs the host's file that gives the resolution of our cluster name:

```
config.vm.provision :shell, :inline => "apt-get update"
```

This updates all the packages in the apt-get cache within the Ubuntu installation. Vagrant then proceeds to install the JDK and the base provisioning. Finally it invokes the application provisioning.

 The base VM image could contain the entire base provisioning already, thus making this portion of the provisioning unrequired. However, it is important to understand the process of creating an appropriate base image and also to balance the amount of specialization in the base images you control; otherwise, they will proliferate.

Creating a Storm cluster – provisioning Storm

Once you have a base set of virtual machines that are ready for application provisioning, you need to install and configure the appropriate packages on each node.

How to do it...

1. Create a new project named `storm-puppet` with the following folder structure:

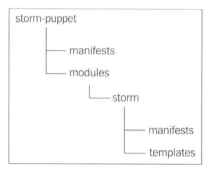

2. The entry point into the Puppet execution on the provisioned node is `site.pp`. Create it in the `manifests` folder:

```
node 'storm.nimbus' {
  $cluster = 'storm1'
  include storm::nimbus
  include storm::ui
}

node /storm.supervisor[1-9]/ {
  $cluster = 'storm1'
  include storm::supervisor
}

node /storm.zookeeper[1-9]/ {
  include storm::zoo
}
```

3. Next, you need to define the storm module. A module exists in the `modules` folder and has its own `manifests` and `template` folder structure, much as with the structure found at the root level of the Puppet project. Within the storm module, create the required manifests (`modules/storm/manifests`), starting with the `init.pp` file:

```
class storm {
  include storm::install
  include storm::config
}
```

4. The installation of the Storm application is the same on each `storm` node; only the configurations are adjusted where required, via templating. Next create the `install.pp` file, which will download the required binaries and install them:

```
class storm::install {

  $BASE_URL="https://bitbucket.org/qanderson/storm-deb-
                    packaging/downloads/"
  $ZMQ_FILE="libzmq0_2.1.7_amd64.deb"
  $JZMQ_FILE="libjzmq_2.1.7_amd64.deb"
  $STORM_FILE="storm_0.8.1_all.deb"

  package { "wget": ensure => latest }

  # call fetch for each file
  exec { "wget_storm":
    command => "/usr/bin/wget ${BASE_URL}${STORM_FILE}" }
  exec {"wget_zmq":
    command => "/usr/bin/wget ${BASE_URL}${ZMQ_FILE}" }
  exec { "wget_jzmq":
    command => "/usr/bin/wget ${BASE_URL}${JZMQ_FILE}" }

  #call package for each file
  package { "libzmq0":
    provider => dpkg,
    ensure => installed,
    source => "${ZMQ_FILE}",
    require => Exec['wget_zmq']
  }
  #call package for each file
  package { "libjzmq":
    provider => dpkg,
    ensure => installed,
    source => "${JZMQ_FILE}",
    require => [Exec['wget_jzmq'],Package['libzmq0']]
  }
  #call package for each file
  package { "storm":
    provider => dpkg,
    ensure => installed,
    source => "${STORM_FILE}",
    require => [Exec['wget_storm'], Package['libjzmq']]
  }
}
```

The `install` manifest here assumes the existence of package, Debian packages, for Ubuntu. These were built using scripts and can be tweaked based on your requirements. The binaries and creation scripts can be found at `https://bitbucket.org/qanderson/storm-deb-packaging`.

The installation consists of the following packages:

- Storm
- ZeroMQ: `http://www.zeromq.org/`
- Java-ZeroMQ

5. The configuration of each node is done through the template-based generation of the configuration files. In the `storm` manifests, create `config.pp`:

```
class storm::config {
  require storm::install
  include storm::params
  file { '/etc/storm/storm.yaml':
    require => Package['storm'],
    content => template('storm/storm.yaml.erb'),
    owner   => 'root',
    group   => 'root',
    mode    => '0644'
  }
  file { '/etc/default/storm':
    require => Package['storm'],
    content => template('storm/default.erb'),
    owner   => 'root',
    group   => 'root',
    mode    => '0644'
  }
}
```

6. All the `storm` parameters are defined using Hiera, with the Hiera configuration invoked from `params.pp` in the `storm` manifests:

```
class storm::params {
  #_ STORM DEFAULTS _#
  $java_library_path = hiera_array('java_library_path',
    ['/usr/local/lib', '/opt/local/lib', '/usr/lib'])
}
```

Due to the sheer number of properties, the file has been concatenated. For the complete file, please refer to the Git repository at `https://bitbucket.org/qanderson/storm-puppet/src`.

7. Each class of node is then specified; here we will specify the `nimbus` class:

```
class storm::nimbus {
  require storm::install
  include storm::config
  include storm::params

  # Install nimbus /etc/default
  storm::service { 'nimbus':
    start      => 'yes',
    jvm_memory => $storm::params::nimbus_mem
  }

}
```

Specify the `supervisor` class:

```
class storm::supervisor {
  require storm::install
  include storm::config
  include storm::params

  # Install supervisor /etc/default
  storm::service { 'supervisor':
    start      => 'yes',
    jvm_memory => $storm::params::supervisor_mem
  }

}
```

Specify the `ui` class:

```
class storm::ui {
  require storm::install
  include storm::config
  include storm::params
  # Install ui /etc/default
  storm::service { 'ui':
    start      => 'yes',
    jvm_memory => $storm::params::ui_mem
  }

}
```

And finally, specify the `zoo` class (for a `zookeeper` node):

```
class storm::zoo {
  package {['zookeeper','zookeeper-bin','zookeeperd']:
    ensure => latest,
  }
}
```

8. Once all the files have been created, initialize the Git repository and push it to `bitbucket.org`.

9. In order to actually run the provisioning, navigate to the `vagrant-storm-cluster` folder and run the following command:

   vagrant up

10. If you would like to `ssh` into any of the nodes, simply specify the following command:

    vagrant ssh nimbus

    Replace `nimbus` with your required node name.

How it works...

There are various patterns that can be applied when using Puppet. The simplest one is using a distributed model, whereby nodes provision themselves as opposed to a centralized model using **Puppet Master**. In the distributed model, updating server configuration simply requires that you update your provisioning manifests and push them to your central Git repository. The various nodes will then pull and apply this configuration. This can either be achieved through cron jobs, triggers, or through the use of a Continuous Delivery tool such as Jenkins, Bamboo, or Go. Provisioning in the development environment is explicitly invoked by Vagrant through the following command:

```
config.vm.provision :shell, :inline => "puppet apply /tmp/storm-puppet/
manifests/site.pp --verbose --modulepath=/tmp/storm-puppet/modules/
--debug"
```

The manifest is then applied declaratively by the Puppet. Puppet is declarative, in that each language element specifies the desired state together with methods for getting there. This means that, when the system is already in the required state, that particular provisioning step will be skipped, together with the adverse effects of duplicate provisioning.

The `storm-puppet` project is therefore cloned onto the node and then the manifest is applied locally. Each node only applies provisioning for itself, based on the hostname specified in the `site.pp` manifest, for example:

```
node 'storm.nimbus' {
  $cluster = 'storm1'
  include storm::nimbus
  include storm::ui
}
```

In this case, the `nimbus` node will include the Hiera configurations for `cluster1`, and the installation for the `nimbus` and `ui` nodes will be performed. Any combination of classes can be included in the `node` definition, thus allowing the complete environment to be succinctly defined.

Deriving basic click statistics

The click topology is designed to gather basic website-usage statistics, specifically:

- ▶ The number of visitors
- ▶ The number of unique visitors
- ▶ The number of visitors for a given country
- ▶ The number of visitors for a given city
- ▶ The percentage of visitors for each city in a given country

The system assumes a limited possible visitor population and prefers server-side client keys as opposed to client-side cookies. The topology derives the geographic information from the IP address and a public IP resolution service.

The click topology also uses **Redis** to store click events being sent into the topology, specifically as a persistent queue, and it also leverages Redis in order to persistently recall the previous visitors to the site.

 For more information on Redis, please visit `Redis.io`.

Getting ready

Before you proceed, you must install Redis (Version 2.6 or greater):

```
wget http://download.redis.io/redis-stable.tar.gz
tar xvzf redis-stable.tar.gz
cd redis-stable
make
sudo cp redis-server /usr/local/bin/
sudo cp redis-cli /usr/local/bin/
```

Then start the Redis server.

How to do it...

1. Create a new Java project named `click-topology`, and create the `pom.xml` file and folder structure as per the "Hello World" topology project.

2. In the `pom.xml` file, update the project name and references, and then add the following dependencies to the `<dependencies>` tag:

```
<dependency>
    <groupId>junit</groupId>
    <artifactId>junit</artifactId>
    <version>4.11</version>
    <scope>test</scope>
</dependency>
<dependency>
    <groupId>org.jmock</groupId>
    <artifactId>jmock-junit4</artifactId>
    <version>2.5.1</version>
    <scope>test</scope>
</dependency>
<dependency>
    <groupId>org.jmock</groupId>
    <artifactId>jmock-legacy</artifactId>
    <version>2.5.1</version>
    <scope>test</scope>
</dependency>
<dependency>
    <groupId>redis.clients</groupId>
    <artifactId>jedis</artifactId>
    <version>2.1.0</version>
</dependency>
```

3. Take a special note of the `scope` definitions of JUnit and JMock so as to not include them in your final deployable JAR.

4. In the `source/main/java` folder, create the `ClickTopology` main class in the `package storm.cookbook` package. This class defines the topology and provides the mechanisms to launch the topology into a cluster or in a local mode. Create the class as follows:

```
public ClickTopology(){
    builder.setSpout("clickSpout", new ClickSpout(), 10);

    //First layer of bolts
    builder.setBolt("repeatsBolt", new RepeatVisitBolt(), 10)
            .shuffleGrouping("clickSpout");
```

```
builder.setBolt("geographyBolt", new GeographyBolt(new
          HttpIPResolver()), 10)
          .shuffleGrouping("clickSpout");

//second layer of bolts, commutative in nature
builder.setBolt("totalStats", new VisitStatsBolt(),
               1).globalGrouping("repeatsBolt");
builder.setBolt("geoStats", new GeoStatsBolt(),
               10).fieldsGrouping("geographyBolt", new
Fields(storm.cookbook.Fields.COUNTRY));
conf.put(Conf.REDIS_PORT_KEY, DEFAULT_JEDIS_PORT);
}
public void runLocal(int runTime){
   conf.setDebug(true);
   conf.put(Conf.REDIS_HOST_KEY, "localhost");
   cluster = new LocalCluster();
   cluster.submitTopology("test", conf,
                       builder.createTopology());
   if(runTime > 0){
       Utils.sleep(runTime);
       shutDownLocal();
   }
}

public void shutDownLocal(){
   if(cluster != null){
       cluster.killTopology("test");
       cluster.shutdown();
   }
}

  public void runCluster(String name, String redisHost)
                      throws AlreadyAliveException,
                      InvalidTopologyException {
     conf.setNumWorkers(20);
     conf.put(Conf.REDIS_HOST_KEY, redisHost);
     StormSubmitter.submitTopology(name, conf,
         builder.createTopology());
  }
```

5. This is followed by the `main` method, which is guided by the number of arguments passed at runtime:

```
public static void main(String[] args) throws Exception {
    ClickTopology topology = new ClickTopology();

    if(args!=null && args.length > 1) {
        topology.runCluster(args[0], args[1]);
    } else {
        if(args!=null && args.length == 1)
            System.out.println("Running in local mode,
                    redis ip missing for cluster run");
        topology.runLocal(10000);
    }

}
```

6. The topology assumes that the web server pushes messages onto a Redis queue. You must create a spout to inject these into the Storm cluster as a stream. In the `storm.cookbook` package, create the `ClickSpout` class, which connects to Redis when it is opened by the cluster:

```
public class ClickSpout extends BaseRichSpout {

    public static Logger LOG =
                Logger.getLogger(ClickSpout.class);

    private Jedis jedis;
    private String host;
    private int port;
    private SpoutOutputCollector collector;


    @Override
    public void declareOutputFields(OutputFieldsDeclarer
        outputFieldsDeclarer) {
        outputFieldsDeclarer.declare(new
          Fields(storm.cookbook.Fields.IP,
                storm.cookbook.Fields.URL,
                storm.cookbook.Fields.CLIENT_KEY));
    }

    @Override
    public void open(Map conf, TopologyContext
                    topologyContext, SpoutOutputCollector
```

```
        spoutOutputCollector) {
    host = conf.get(Conf.REDIS_HOST_KEY).toString();
    port = Integer.valueOf(conf
        .get(Conf.REDIS_PORT_KEY).toString());
    this.collector = spoutOutputCollector;
    connectToRedis();
}

private void connectToRedis() {
    jedis = new Jedis(host, port);
}
```

7. The cluster will then poll the spout for new tuples through the `nextTuple` method:

```
public void nextTuple() {
  String content = jedis.rpop("count");
  if(content==null || "nil".equals(content)) {
    try { Thread.sleep(300); }
    catch (InterruptedException e) {}
  } else {
    JSONObject obj=(JSONObject) JSONValue.parse(content);
    String ip = obj.get(storm.cookbook.Fields.IP).toString();
    String url = obj.get(storm.cookbook.Fields.URL).toString();
    String clientKey = obj.get(storm.cookbook.Fields.CLIENT_KEY)
                            .toString();
    collector.emit(new Values(ip,url,clientKey));
    }
}
```

8. Next, we need to create the bolts that will enrich the basic data through the database or remote API lookups. Let us start with the repeat visit bolt. This bolt will check the client's ID against previous visit records and emit the enriched tuple with a flag set for unique visits. Create the `RepeatVisitBolt` class, providing the open and Redis connection logic:

```
public class RepeatVisitBolt extends BaseRichBolt {

    private OutputCollector collector;

    private Jedis jedis;
    private String host;
    private int port;

    @Override
```

```
public void prepare(Map conf,
 TopologyContext topologyContext, OutputCollector
 outputCollector) {
     this.collector = outputCollector;
     host = conf.get(Conf.REDIS_HOST_KEY).toString();
     port = Integer.valueOf(conf.
          get(Conf.REDIS_PORT_KEY).toString());
     connectToRedis();
}

private void connectToRedis() {
     jedis = new Jedis(host, port);
     jedis.connect();
}
```

9. In the `execute` method, the tuple from the `ClickSpout` class is provided by the cluster. The bolt needs to look up the previous visit flags from Redis, based on the fields in the tuple, and emit the enriched tuple:

```
public void execute(Tuple tuple) {
  String ip = tuple.getStringByField(storm.cookbook.Fields.IP);
  String clientKey = tuple.getStringByField(storm.cookbook.Fields
                                      .CLIENT_KEY);
  String url = tuple.getStringByField(storm.cookbook.Fields.URL);
  String key = url + ":" + clientKey;
  String value = jedis.get(key);
  if(value == null){
      jedis.set(key, "visited");
      collector.emit(new Values(clientKey, url,
         Boolean.TRUE.toString()));
  } else {
      collector.emit(new Values(clientKey, url,
              Boolean.FALSE.toString()));
  }

}
```

10. Next, the geographic enrichment bolt must be created. This bolt will emit an enriched tuple by looking up the country and city of the client's IP address through a remote API call. The `GeographyBolt` class delegates the actual call to an injected IP resolver in order to increase the testability of the class. In the `storm.cookbook` package, create the `GeographyBolt` class, extending from the `BaseRichBolt` interface, and implement the `execute` method:

```
public void execute(Tuple tuple) {
    String ip = tuple.getStringByField(storm
                  .cookbook.Fields.IP);
    JSONObject json = resolver.resolveIP(ip);
    String city = (String) json.get(storm
                  .cookbook.Fields.CITY);
    String country = (String) json.get(storm
                  .cookbook.Fields.COUNTRY_NAME);
    collector.emit(new Values(country, city));
}
```

11. Provide a resolver by implementing the resolver, `HttpIPResolver`, and injecting it into `GeographyBolt` at design time:

```
public class HttpIPResolver implements IPResolver, Serializable {
    static String url =
            "http://api.hostip.info/get_json.php";
    @Override
    public JSONObject resolveIP(String ip) {
        URL geoUrl = null;
        BufferedReader in = null;
        try {
            geoUrl = new URL(url + "?ip=" + ip);
            URLConnection connection = geoUrl.openConnection();
            in = new BufferedReader(new InputStreamReader(
                              connection.getInputStream()));
            JSONObject json = (JSONObject) JSONValue.parse(in);
            in.close();
            return json;
        } catch (IOException e) {
            e.printStackTrace();
        }
        finally {
            if(in != null){
                try {
                    in.close();
                } catch (IOException e) {}
            }
        }
        return null;
    }
}
```

12. Next, we need to derive the geographic stats. The `GeoStatsBolt` class simply receives the enriched tuple from `GeographicBolt` and maintains an in-memory structure of the data. It also emits the updated counts to any interested party. The `GeoStatsBolt` class is designed such that the total population of the countries can be split between many bolts; however, all cities within each country must arrive at the same bolt. The topology, therefore, splits streams into the bolt on this basis:

```
builder.setBolt("geoStats", new GeoStatsBolt(),
        10).fieldsGrouping("geographyBolt", new
        Fields(storm.cookbook.Fields.COUNTRY));
```

13. Creating the `GeoStatsBolt` class, provide the implementation for the `execute` method:

```
public void execute(Tuple tuple) {
        String country = tuple.getStringByField(storm.cookbook.
Fields.COUNTRY);
        String city = tuple.getStringByField(Fields.CITY);
        if(!stats.containsKey(country)){
            stats.put(country, new CountryStats(country));
        }
        stats.get(country).cityFound(city);
        collector.emit(new Values(country,
            stats.get(country).getCountryTotal(), city,
            stats.get(country).getCityTotal(city)));

}
```

14. The bulk of logic is contained in the inner-model class that maintains an in-memory model of the city and country:

```
private class CountryStats {
        private int countryTotal = 0;
        private static final int COUNT_INDEX = 0;
        private static final int PERCENTAGE_INDEX = 1;
        private String countryName;
        public CountryStats(String countryName){
            this.countryName = countryName;
        }
        private Map<String, List<Integer>> cityStats = new
          HashMap<String, List<Integer>>();
        public void cityFound(String cityName){
            countryTotal++;
            if(cityStats.containsKey(cityName)){
                cityStats.get(cityName).set(COUNT_INDEX,
                  cityStats.get(cityName)
```

```
                            .get(COUNT_INDEX).intValue() + 1);
                } else {
                    List<Integer> list = new
                                    LinkedList<Integer>();
        //add some dummy data
                    list.add(1);
                    list.add(0);
                    cityStats.put(cityName, list);
                }

            double percent = (double)cityStats.get(cityName)
                    .get(COUNT_INDEX)/(double)countryTotal;
            cityStats.get(cityName).set(PERCENTAGE_INDEX,
                    (int)percent);
        }
    public int getCountryTotal(){return countryTotal;}
    public int getCityTotal(String cityName){
        return cityStats.get(cityName)
            .get(COUNT_INDEX).intValue();
    }
}
```

15. Finally, the `VisitorStatsBolt` method provides the final counting functionality for visitors and unique visits, based on the enriched stream from the `RepeatVisitBolt` class. This bolt needs to receive all the count information in order to maintain a single in-memory count, which is reflected in the topology definition:

```
builder.setBolt("totalStats", new VisitStatsBolt(), 1).globalGroup
ing("repeatsBolt");
```

16. In order to implement the `VisitorStatsBolt` class, create the class and define two member-level integers, `total` and `uniqueCount`; then implement the `execute` method:

```
public void execute(Tuple tuple) {
    boolean unique = Boolean.parseBoolean(tuple
     .getStringByField(storm.cookbook.Fields.UNIQUE));
    total++;
    if(unique)uniqueCount++;
    collector.emit(new Values(total,uniqueCount));
    }
```

How it works...

The following diagram illustrates the click topology:

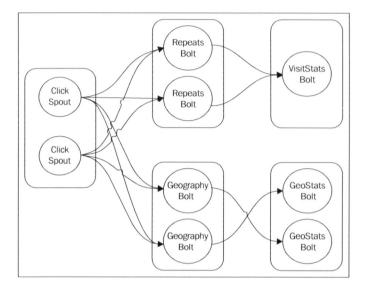

The spout emits the click events from the web server into the topology, through a shuffle grouping, to both the geography and repeat bolts. This ensures that the load is evenly distributed around the cluster, especially for these slow or highly latent processes.

 It is important to understand the commutative versus associative nature of your data model, together with any other concerns that are in your streams and inherent models before designing your topology.

It is important to understand the parallelism of Storm while setting up the topology structure. There is an excellent summary of this on the wiki (`https://github.com/nathanmarz/storm/wiki/Understanding-the-parallelism-of-a-Storm-topology`). The key points to take into account are:

- The number of worker processes for the topology (`TOPOLOGY_WORKERS`).
- The number of executors (threads) per component of the topology. This is set using the parallelism hint. Note that this sets only the initial value (number of threads); this can be increased at runtime using topology rebalancing (through the UI or CLI). You can limit the number of executors using the `Config#setMaxTaskParallelism()` method.
- The number of tasks is set by default to 1 per executor. You can adjust this value when you declare a component, using the `ComponentConfigurationDeclarer#setNumTasks()` method.

These are the key elements to consider when sizing your cluster. The cluster will try distributing work to worker processes, each containing many executors that may be executing one or more tasks. The number of executors per worker is therefore a function of the number of executors over the number of workers. A good example of this can be seen in the previously mentioned wiki page.

Using these numbers, you can size your cluster in terms of nodes and cores per node, where ideally you should have one core per thread (executor) in the cluster.

Unit testing a bolt

Unit testing is an essential part of any delivery; the logic contained in the bolts must also be unit tested.

Getting ready

Unit testing often involves a process called **mocking** that allows you to use dynamically generated fake instances of objects as dependencies in order to ensure that a particular class is tested on a unit basis. This book illustrates unit testing using JUnit 4 and JMock. Please take the time to read up on JMock's recipes online at `http://jmock.org/cookbook.html`.

How to do it...

1. In the `src/test/java` folder, create the `storm.cookbook` package and create the `StormTestCase` class. This class is a simple abstraction of some of the initialization code:

```java
public class StormTestCase {

    protected Mockery context = new Mockery() {{
        setImposteriser(ClassImposteriser.INSTANCE);
    }};


    protected Tuple getTuple(){
        final Tuple tuple = context.mock(Tuple.class);
        return tuple;
    }
}
```

2. Then create the `TestRepeatVisitBolt` class that extends from `StormTestCase`, and mark it with the parameterized runner annotation:

```java
@RunWith(value = Parameterized.class)
public class TestRepeatVisitBold extends StormTestCase {
```

3. The test case logic of the class is contained in a single `execute` method:

```java
public void testExecute(){
        jedis = new Jedis("localhost",6379);
        RepeatVisitBolt bolt = new RepeatVisitBolt();
        Map config = new HashMap();
        config.put("redis-host", "localhost");
        config.put("redis-port", "6379");
        final OutputCollector collector =
                context.mock(OutputCollector.class);
        bolt.prepare(config, null, collector);

        assertEquals(true, bolt.isConnected());

        final Tuple tuple = getTuple();
        context.checking(new Expectations(){{
           oneOf(tuple).getStringByField(Fields
                  IP);will(returnValue(ip));
           oneOf(tuple).getStringByField(Fields
                  .CLIENT_KEY);will(returnValue(clientKey));
           oneOf(tuple).getStringByField(Fields
                  .URL);will(returnValue(url));
          oneOf(collector).emit(new Values
                  (clientKey, url, expected));
        }});

        bolt.execute(tuple);
        context.assertIsSatisfied();

        if(jedis != null)
              jedis.disconnect();
      }
```

4. Next, the parameters must be defined:

```java
@Parameterized.Parameters
   public static Collection<Object[]> data() {
      Object[][] data = new Object[][] {
         { "192.168.33.100", "Client1", "myintranet.com", "false" },
         { "192.168.33.100", "Client1", "myintranet.com", "false" },
         { "192.168.33.101", "Client2", "myintranet1.com", "true" },
         { "192.168.33.102", "Client3", "myintranet2.com", false"}};
   return Arrays.asList(data);
   }
```

5. The base provisioning of the values must be done before the tests using Redis:

```
@BeforeClass
    public static void setupJedis(){
        Jedis jedis = new Jedis("localhost",6379);
        jedis.flushDB();
        Iterator<Object[]> it = data().iterator();
        while(it.hasNext()){
            Object[] values = it.next();
            if(values[3].equals("false")){
                String key = values[2] + ":" + values[1];
                jedis.set(key, "visited");//unique, meaning
                                          it must exist
            }
        }
    }
```

 It is always useful to leave data in the stack after the test completes in order to review and debug, clearing again only on the next run.

How it works...

Firstly, the unit test works by defining a set of test data. This allows us to test many different cases without unnecessary abstractions or duplication. Before the tests execute, the static data is populated into the Redis DB, thus allowing the tests to run deterministically. The test method is then executed once per line of parameterized data; many different cases are verified.

JMock provides mock instances of the collector and the tuples to be emitted by the bolt. The expected behavior is then defined in terms of these mocked objects and their interactions:

```
context.checking(new Expectations(){{
oneOf(tuple).getStringByField(Fields.IP);will(returnValue(ip));
oneOf(tuple).getStringByField(Fields.CLIENT_KEY);will(returnValue(
                                                     clientKey));
oneOf(tuple).getStringByField(Fields.URL);will(returnValue(url));
oneOf(collector).emit(new Values(clientKey, url, expected));
        }});
```

Although these are separate lines of code, within the bounds of the expectations they should be read declaratively. I expect the `getStringField` method of the tuple to be called exactly once with the value `ip`, and the mock object must then return a value to the class being tested.

This mechanism provides a clean way to exercise the bolt.

 There are many different kinds of unit tests; often it becomes necessary to test against a DB in such a manner; if you can help it, rather mock out all dependencies of the class and implement a true unit test. This would be possible with the geography bolt due to the `resolver` abstraction.

Implementing an integration test

Integration testing can mean many different things depending on the situation and audience. For the purposes of this book, integration testing is a means of testing the topology from end-to-end, with defined input and output points within a local cluster. This allows for a full-functional verification of the functionality before deploying it to an actual cluster.

How to do it...

1. Create the `IntegrationTestTopology` class in the `src/test/java` folder in the `storm.cookbook` package. Set up a local topology by adding in a testing utility bolt:

```
@BeforeClass
    public static void setup(){
    //We want all output tuples coming to the mock for
    // testing purposes
      topology.getBuilder().setBolt("testBolt",testBolt, 1)
                          .globalGrouping("geoStats")
                          .globalGrouping("totalStats");
    // run in local mode, but we will shut the cluster down
    // when we are finished
        topology.runLocal(0);
    //jedis required for input and output of the cluster
        jedis = new Jedis("localhost",
      Integer.parseInt(ClickTopology.DEFAULT_JEDIS_PORT));
        jedis.connect();
        jedis.flushDB();
    //give it some time to startup before running the tests.
        Utils.sleep(5000);
    }
```

2. Then, define the expected parameters as a set of arrays arranged in pairs:

```
@Parameterized.Parameters
    public static Collection<Object[]> data() {
    Object[][] data = new Object[][] { {new Object[]{
 "165.228.250.178", "internal.com",  "Client1"}, //input
```

```
        new Object[]{ "AUSTRALIA", new Long(1), "SYDNEY", new Long(1),
                new Long(1), new Long(1) } },//expectations
            {new Object[]{ "165.228.250.178", "internal.com",
                        "Client1"}, //input
        new Object[]{ "AUSTRALIA", new Long(2), "SYDNEY", new
                        Long(2), new Long(2), new Long(1) } },
            {new Object[]{ "4.17.136.0", "internal.com",
                        "Client1"}, //input, same client,
                        different location
            new Object[]{ "UNITED STATES", new Long(1), "DERRY,
                        NH", new Long(1), new Long(3), new
                        Long(1) } },
            {new Object[]{ "4.17.136.0", "internal.com",
                        "Client2"}, //input, same client,
                        different location
            new Object[]{ "UNITED STATES", new Long(2), "DERRY,
                        NH", new Long(2), new Long(4), new
                        Long(2) } }};//expectations
        return Arrays.asList(data);
    }
Object[] input;
    Object[] expected;
    public IntegrationTestTopology(Object[] input,Object[]
                                    expected){
    this.input = input;
    this.expected = expected;
    }
```

3. The test logic can then be based on these parameters:

```
@Test
    public void inputOutputClusterTest(){
        JSONObject content = new JSONObject();
        content.put("ip" ,input[0]);
        content.put("url" ,input[1]);
        content.put("clientKey" ,input[2]);

        jedis.rpush("count", content.toJSONString());

        Utils.sleep(3000);

        int count = 0;
        String data = jedis.rpop("TestTuple");

        while(data != null){
          JSONArray values = (JSONArray)
                            JSONValue.parse(data);

            if(values.get(0).toString().contains("geoStats")){
              count++;
```

```
                    assertEquals(expected[0],
                    values.get(1).toString().toUpperCase());
                    assertEquals(expected[1], values.get(2));
                    assertEquals(expected[2],
                    values.get(3).toString().toUpperCase());
                    assertEquals(expected[3], values.get(4));
                } else if(values.get(0).toString().
    contains("totalStats")) {
                        count++;
                        assertEquals(expected[4], values.get(1));
                        assertEquals(expected[5], values.get(2));
                }
                data = jedis.rpop("TestTuple");


        }
            assertEquals(2, count);


    }
```

How it works...

The integration test works by creating a local cluster and then injecting input values into the cluster through Redis, in the same way as a real web server would for the given design. It then adds a specific testing bolt to the end of the topology that receives all the output tuples and tests these against the expected values.

Once the `TestBolt` value is submitted to the cluster, it is no longer accessible from the test; therefore, the outputs can only be accessed through persistence. `TestBolt` persists received tuples to Redis, where the test case can read and validate them. The logic within `TestBolt` is as follows:

```
public void execute(Tuple input) {
    List objects = input.getValues();
    objects.add(0, input.getSourceComponent());
    jedis.rpush("TestTuple", JSONArray.toJSONString(objects));


}
```

This is then read by the test and validated against the expected values:

```
String data = jedis.rpop("TestTuple");

    while(data != null){
        JSONArray values = (JSONArray) JSONValue.parse(data);
```

```
    if(values.get(0).toString().contains("geoStats")){
      count++;
        assertEquals(expected[0], values.get(1)
                       .toString().toUpperCase());
        assertEquals(expected[1], values.get(2));
        assertEquals(expected[2], values.get(3)
                       .toString().toUpperCase());
        assertEquals(expected[3], values.get(4));
    } else if(values.get(0).toString().contains("totalStats"))
    {
    count++;
        assertEquals(expected[4], values.get(1));
        assertEquals(expected[5], values.get(2));
    }
    data = jedis.rpop("TestTuple");

  }
    assertEquals(2, count);

}
```

Deploying to the cluster

The final step in the development process is to functionally test the topology in a cluster before promoting it to the next environment.

How to do it...

1. First you need to configure the Storm client on your host development machine by creating the `.storm` folder in your user home directory. Create `storm.yaml` in this folder with the following content:

```
storm.local.dir: "/mnt/storm"
nimbus.host: "192.168.33.100"
```

2. Package your topology using the following command within the project's root:

   mvn package

3. This will produce a completely packaged JAR in the target folder of the project. You can deploy this to the cluster using the `storm` client command:

   storm jar jarName.jar [TopologyName] [Args]

How it works...

The `storm` command-line client provides you with all the tools you need to control the cluster's functionality. Part of this is the ability to deploy packaged topologies. For more information on the storm CLI, please review the detailed documentation on the wiki at `https://github.com/nathanmarz/storm/wiki/Command-line-client`.

2
Log Stream Processing

In this chapter we will cover:

- ▶ Creating a log agent
- ▶ Creating the log spout
- ▶ Rule-based analysis of the log stream
- ▶ Indexing and persisting the log data
- ▶ Counting and persisting log statistics
- ▶ Creating an integration test for the log stream cluster
- ▶ Creating a log analytics dashboard

Introduction

This chapter will present an implementation recipe for an enterprise log storage and a search and analysis solution based on the Storm processor. Log data processing isn't necessarily a problem that needs solving again; it is, however, a good analogy.

Stream processing is a key architectural concern in the modern enterprise; however, streams of data are often semi-structured at best. By presenting an approach to enterprise log processing, this chapter is designed to provide the reader with all the key elements to achieve this level of capability on any kind of data. Log data is also extremely convenient in an academic setting given its sheer abundance. A key success factor for any stream processing or analytics effort is a deep understanding of the actual data and sourcing data can often be difficult.

It is, therefore, important that the reader considers how the architectural blueprint could be applied to other forms of data within the enterprise.

The following diagram illustrates all the elements that we will develop in this chapter:

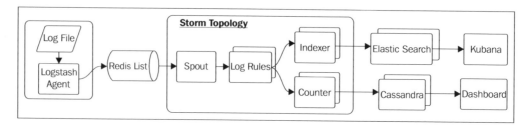

You will learn how to create a log agent that can be distributed across all the nodes in your environment. You will also learn to collect these log entries centrally using Storm and Redis, and then analyze, index, and count the logs, such that we will be able to search them later and display base statistics for them.

Creating a log agent

Modern enterprise architectures consist of a huge number of solutions, each comprising many nodes. Some MapReduce clusters contain hundreds of nodes. Each node contains an array of applications and services, both at the operating system and Application layers. These services and applications generate varying volumes of log data. There is an increasing recognition of the importance of log data within the enterprise community for the following reasons:

- It is a key source of information for any IT operations team to maintain available systems

- It is key to finding and resolving problems, both in the production and systems testing phases

- It is increasingly becoming a source of business value, where valuable business data is trapped in this semi-structured data, including:

  - Risk and compliance data
  - Business operational data
  - Web analytics
  - Security
  - Financial forecasts

In order to leverage valuable log data, it must be sourced from these nodes and delivered securely and easily to a centralized log service for storage, indexing, and analysis. This recipe demonstrates how to achieve this through an open source log agent called **logstash**.

There are many good commercial and open source log solutions available. This chapter uses portions of logstash; further logstash recipes can be found at http://cookbook.logstash.net/ and http://logstash.net/docs/1.1.13/tutorials/getting-started-centralized. A good commercial equivalent is Splunk (http://www.splunk.com/).

How to do it...

1. To start, the logs on your local node will be streamed into the topology. Start by downloading and configuring logstash as follows:

   wget https://logstash.objects.dreamhost.com/release/logstash-1.1.7-monolithic.jar

2. Then, using your favorite text editor, create a file called `shipper.conf` containing the following:

   ```
   input {
     file {
       type => "syslog"

       # Wildcards work here :)
       path => [ "/var/log/messages", "/var/log/system.*", "/var/
                 log/*.log" ]
     }
   }

   output {
     # Output events to stdout for debugging. Feel free to remove
     # this output if you don't need it.
     stdout { }

     redis {
       host => "localhost"
       data_type => "list"
       key => "rawLogs"
     }
   }
   ```

3. After starting a local instance of Redis, you can start this logging agent by issuing the following command:

   java -jar logstash-1.1.7-monolithic.jar -f shipper.conf

How it works...

logstash implements a very simple model of input-filter-output with an ever-expanding list of plugins for any of these three elements. The preceding configuration file (`shipper.conf`) configures at least one input and output.

The file input plugin will tail files based on filenames or wildcards in the specified paths. Many file inputs can be configured, each with a different type. The log type is important for later processing and categorization. As we have not configured any filters in this configuration file, the raw log will be passed to the output plugin. The output plugin is the Redis plugin that will output the log to the Redis instance on localhost to a list called `rawLogs`.

logstash can easily be included in the baseline provisioning of each node provisioned on your infrastructure, including key exchange for secure log delivery via any transport mechanism you are comfortable with.

Creating the log spout

The log topology will read all logs through the Redis channel that is fed by logstash; these logs will be emitted into the topology through the spout described in this recipe. As this is a new topology, we must first create the new topology project.

How to do it...

Start by creating the project directory and the standard Maven folder structure (`http://maven.apache.org/guides/introduction/introduction-to-the-standard-directory-layout.html`).

1. Create the POM as per the *Creating a "Hello World" topology* recipe in *Chapter 1, Setting Up Your Development Environment*, updating the `<artifactId>` and `<name>` tag values and including the following dependencies:

```
<dependency>
        <groupId>junit</groupId>
        <artifactId>junit</artifactId>
        <version>4.11</version>
        <scope>test</scope>
</dependency>
<dependency>
        <groupId>org.slf4j</groupId>
        <artifactId>slf4j-log4j12</artifactId>
        <version>1.6.1</version>
</dependency>
<dependency>
```

```xml
            <groupId>org.jmock</groupId>
            <artifactId>jmock-legacy</artifactId>
            <version>2.5.1</version>
            <scope>test</scope>
</dependency>
<dependency>
            <groupId>storm</groupId>
            <artifactId>storm</artifactId>
            <version>0.8.1</version>
          <!-- keep storm out of the jar-with-dependencies -->
            <scope>provided</scope>
            <exclusions>
               <exclusion>
                  <artifactId>slf4j-api</artifactId>
                  <groupId>org.slf4j</groupId>
               </exclusion>
            </exclusions>
</dependency>
<dependency>
            <groupId>com.googlecode.json-simple</groupId>
            <artifactId>json-simple</artifactId>
            <version>1.1</version>
</dependency>
<dependency>
            <groupId>redis.clients</groupId>
            <artifactId>jedis</artifactId>
            <version>2.1.0</version>
</dependency>
<dependency>
            <groupId>commons-httpclient</groupId>
            <artifactId>commons-httpclient</artifactId>
            <version>3.1</version>
</dependency>
<dependency>
            <groupId>org.jmock</groupId>
            <artifactId>jmock-junit4</artifactId>
            <version>2.5.1</version>
            <scope>test</scope>
</dependency>
<dependency>
            <groupId>com.github.ptgoetz</groupId>
            <artifactId>storm-cassandra</artifactId>
            <version>0.3.1-SNAPSHOT</version>
</dependency>
```

```
<dependency>
        <groupId>org.elasticsearch</groupId>
        <artifactId>elasticsearch</artifactId>
        <version>0.20.2</version>
</dependency>
<dependency>
        <groupId>org.drools</groupId>
        <artifactId>drools-core</artifactId>
        <version>5.5.0.Final</version>
</dependency>
<dependency>
        <groupId>org.drools</groupId>
        <artifactId>drools-compiler</artifactId>
        <version>5.5.0.Final</version>
</dependency>
</dependencies>
```

2. Import the project into Eclipse after generating the Eclipse project files as follows:

   `mvn eclipse:eclipse`

3. Tuples in the log topology will carry a log domain object that encapsulates the data and parsing logic for a single log record or an entry in a logfile. In the created project, create this domain object:

```
public class LogEntry {
    public static Logger LOG = Logger.getLogger(LogEntry.class);
    private String source;
    private String type;
    private List<String> tags = new ArrayList<String>();
    private Map<String,String> fields = new HashMap<String,
                                        String>();
    private Date timestamp;
    private String sourceHost;
    private String sourcePath;
    private String message = "";
    private boolean filter = false;
    private NotificationDetails notifyAbout = null;
    private static String[] FORMATS = new String[]{"yyyy-MM-
dd'T'HH:mm:ss.SSS",
        "yyyy.MM.dd G 'at' HH:mm:ss z",
        "yyyyy.MMMMM.dd GGG hh:mm aaa",
        "EEE, d MMM yyyy HH:mm:ss Z",
        "yyMMddHHmmssZ"};
```

```
@SuppressWarnings("unchecked")
public LogEntry(JSONObject json){
    source = (String)json.get("@source");
    timestamp =
            parseDate((String)json.get("@timestamp"));
    sourceHost = (String)json.get("@source_host");
    sourcePath = (String)json.get("@source_path");
    message = (String)json.get("@message");
    type = (String)json.get("@type");

    JSONArray array = (JSONArray)json.get("@tags");
    tags.addAll(array);
    JSONObject fields = (JSONObject)json.get("@fields");
    fields.putAll(fields);
}

public Date parseDate(String value){
    SimpleDateFormat format = new
            SimpleDateFormat(FORMATS[i]);
    for(int i = 0; i < FORMATS.length; i++){
        Date temp;
        try {
            temp = format.parse(value);
            if(temp != null)
                return temp;
        } catch (ParseException e) {}
    }
    LOG.error("Could not parse timestamp for log");
    return null;
}

@SuppressWarnings("unchecked")
public JSONObject toJSON(){
    JSONObject json = new JSONObject();
    json.put("@source", source);
    json.put("@timestamp",DateFormat
            .getDateInstance().format(timestamp));
    json.put("@source_host",sourceHost);
    json.put("@source_path",sourcePath);
```

```
json.put("@message",message);
json.put("@type",type);
JSONArray temp = new JSONArray();
temp.addAll(tags);
json.put("@tags", temp);
JSONObject fieldTemp = new JSONObject();
fieldTemp.putAll(fields);
json.put("@fields",fieldTemp);
return json;
} ...
```

The `getter`, `setter`, and `equals` methods have been excluded
from this code snippet; however, they must be implemented in order.
The `equals` method is vital for unit testing purposes.

4. Then create the `Logspout` class that extends the `BaseRichSpout` interface
    and implements the same pattern as described in *Chapter 1, Setting Up Your
    Development Environment*, declaring a single field as follows:

```
outputFieldsDeclarer.declare(new Fields(FieldNames.LOG_ENTRY));
```

And then emitting the received log entries into the topology as follows:

```
public void nextTuple() {
    String content = jedis.rpop(LOG_CHANNEL);
    if(content==null || "nil".equals(content)) {
     //sleep to prevent starving other threads
        try { Thread.sleep(300); }
        catch (InterruptedException e) {}
    } else {
        JSONObject obj=(JSONObject)
                    JSONValue.parse(content);
        LogEntry entry = new LogEntry(obj);
         collector.emit(new Values(entry));
    }
}
```

Literals should be avoided in the code as far as possible; tuples allow
for effective runtime coupling; however, peppering code with field name
literals for elements that are effectively coupled prior to runtime doesn't
add any value. Hence the usage of static field name definitions.

How it works...

The Redis spout implementation is already familiar; the key logic implemented in this recipe is the parsing logic within the domain object of the `LogEntry` class. logstash submits log lines as separate JSON values into the Redis channel. These JSON values are in the following format:

```
{
"@source":"file://PATH",
"@tags":[],
"@fields":{},
"@timestamp":"yyyy-MM-ddThh:mm:ss.SSS",
"@source_host":"hostname",
"@source_path":"path",
"@message":"Syslog log line contents",
"@type":"syslog"
}
```

There's more...

The JSON format provides for two key structures, namely the JSON object and the JSON array. The JSON website (`www.json.org`) provides a concise definition of each and has also been provided here for the sake of convenience. An **object** is an unordered set of name/value pairs. An object begins with { (left brace) and ends with } (right brace). Each name is followed by : (colon) and the name/value pairs are separated by , (comma).

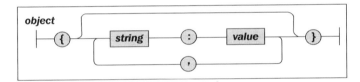

An **array** is an ordered collection of values. An array begins with [(left bracket) and ends with] (right bracket). The values are separated by , (comma).

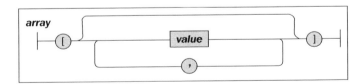

A **value** can be a string in double quotes; a number; true, false, or null; an object; or an array. These structures can be nested.

The constructor of the `LogEntry` object takes `JSONObject` as the only parameter and initializes its internal values based on the contained values. The `LogEntry` object is also able to convert itself into a `JSONObject` through the `toJSON()` method, which will become useful later. `LogEntry` makes heavy use of the `com.googlecode.json-simple` library in order to achieve the first level of parsing from string to a workable structure.

Although the structure is well-defined, the date-time format can vary. The `parseDate()` method, therefore, provides a best-effort approach to parse the date. A static list of supported date-time formats is defined as the `FORMATS` class member variable.

Rule-based analysis of the log stream

Any reasonable log management system needs to be able to achieve the following:

▸ Filter logs that aren't important, and therefore should not be counted or stored. These often include log entries at the `INFO` or `DEBUG` levels (yes, these exist in production systems).

▸ Analyze the log entry further and extract as much meaning and new fields as possible.

▸ Enhance/update the log entry prior to storage.

▸ Send notifications on when certain logs are received.

▸ Correlate log events to derive new meaning.

▸ Deal with changes in the log's structure and formatting.

This recipe integrates the JBoss Library and Drools into a bolt to make these goals easily achievable in a declarative and clear manner. Drools is an open source implementation of a forward-chaining rules engine that is able to infer new values and execute the logic based on matching logic. You can find more details on the Drools project at `http://www.jboss.org/drools/`.

How to do it...

1. Within Eclipse, create a class called `LogRulesBolt`, which extends `BaseRichBolt`, within the `storm.cookbook.log` package. As with the `LogSpout` class, the `LogRulesBolt` class will emit a single value containing a `LogEntry` instance.

   ```
   declarer.declare(new Fields(FieldNames.LOG_ENTRY));
   ```

2. Add a private member-level variable `ksession` of the `StatelessKnowledgeSession` class and initialize it within the bolt's `prepare` method.

   ```
   KnowledgeBuilder kbuilder = KnowledgeBuilderFactory.
   newKnowledgeBuilder();
   ```

```
kbuilder.add( ResourceFactory.newClassPathResource(
            "/Syslog.drl", getClass() ), ResourceType.DRL );
if ( kbuilder.hasErrors() ) {
    LOG.error( kbuilder.getErrors().toString() );
}
KnowledgeBase kbase = KnowledgeBaseFactory.
newKnowledgeBase();
kbase.addKnowledgePackages( kbuilder.getKnowledgePackages()
);
ksession = kbase.newStatelessKnowledgeSession();
```

> The initialization of this knowledge session includes only a single set of rules for the `syslog` logs. It is recommended that rules management be extracted out into Drools Guvnor, or similar, and rules resources be retrieved via an agent. This is outside the scope of this book but more details are available at the following link:
>
> `http://www.jboss.org/drools/drools-guvnor.html`

3. In the bolt's `execute` method, you need to pass the `LogEntry` object from the tuple into the knowledge session.

```
LogEntry entry = (LogEntry)input.getValueByField(FieldNames.LOG_
ENTRY);
    if(entry == null){
        LOG.fatal( "Received null or incorrect value from
                    tuple" );
        return;
    }
    ksession.execute( entry );
    if(!entry.isFilter()){
        collector.emit(new Values(entry));
    }
```

4. You next need to create the rules resource file; this can simply be done with a text editor or using the Eclipse plugin available from the update site (`http://download.jboss.org/drools/release/5.5.0.Final/org.drools.updatesite/`). The rules resource file should be placed at the root of the classpath; create the file named `Syslog.drl` in `src/main/resources` and add this folder to the build path within Eclipse by right-clicking on the folder and going to **Build Path | Use as source folder**.

5. Add the following content to the rules resource:

```
package storm.cookbook.log.rules

import storm.cookbook.log.model.LogEntry;
```

```
import java.util.regex.Matcher
import java.util.regex.Pattern

rule "Host Correction"

    when
        l: LogEntry(sourceHost == "localhost")
    then
        l.setSourceHost("localhost.example.com");

end

rule "Filter By Type"
    when
        l: LogEntry(type != "syslog")
    then
        l.setFilter(true);
end

rule "Extract Fields"
    salience 100//run later
    when
        l: LogEntry(filter != true)
    then
        String logEntryPattern = "^([\\d.]+) (\\S+) (\\S+) \\
[(([\\w:/]+\\s[+\\-]\\d{4})\\] \"(.+?)\" (\\d{3}) (\\d+)
\"([^\"]+)\" \"([^\"]+)\"";
        Matcher matcher = Pattern.compile(logEntryPattern).
matcher(l.getMessage());
        if(matcher.find()){
            l.addField("_pid",matcher.group(1));
            l.addField("_src",matcher.group(2));
        }
end
```

How it works...

Drools supports two types of knowledge sessions, namely **stateful** and **stateless**. For this use case, a stateless session is all that is required.

> Stateful sessions are always to be used with caution as they can lead to performance problems. They essentially maintain facts in memory between session executions. There are use cases where this is vital; however, the nature of a forward-chaining rete engine is that it will degrade in performance exponentially as facts are added to its knowledge base.

A knowledge session is used to evaluate facts against a known set of rules. This is set up within the `prepare` method of the bolt, with the rules provided at that point. Within the execution of the bolt, `LogEntry` is extracted from the tuple and passed into the knowledge session through the following call:

```
ksession.execute( entry );
```

The knowledge session will act as an entry during execution and we can expect it to be potentially different once the call has completed. Contained within the `LogEntry` object is a control field called `filter`. If a rule sets this to `true`, the log entry is to be dropped; this is implemented by checking prior to emitting a tuple containing the entry after the rules execution.

```
if(!entry.isFilter()){
        collector.emit(new Values(entry));
    }
```

Within the rules resource file, there are three rules currently defined.

- `Host Correction`
- `Filter By Type`
- `Extract Fields`

These rules are implemented for demonstration purposes only and aren't necessarily viable production rules. The `Host Correction` rule tries to correct the host name value such that it is fully qualified. The autonomy of a rule is that, when a matching criterion is met, the result is displayed. The `when` clause of this rule will match against the `LogEntry` instance whose `sourceHost` field is `localhost`.

```
1: LogEntry(sourceHost == "localhost")
```

This clause also assigns any matching instance to a local variable `1` within the scope of this rule. The functionality specified in the `then` clause is simply plain old Java, which is added into the current classpath after compilation at runtime. These rules imply making the `localhost` value fully qualified.

```
1.setSourceHost("localhost.example.com");
```

The `Filter By Type` rule will set the filter to `true` for all entries whose type doesn't match `syslog`.

The `Extract Fields` rule is more interesting. Firstly, because it includes a `salience` value, which ensures it is evaluated last. This ensures that it never extracts fields from filtered logs. It then uses regular expression matching to extract more fields and structure from the logfile. While regular expressions are outside the scope of this book, they are widely understood and well documented.

For completeness's sake, here are some more useful examples of expressions for log entries:

- Match the date: `((?<=>))\w+\x20\d+`

- Match the time: `((?<=\d\x20))\d+:\d+:\d+`

- Match an IP address: `((?<=[,]))(\d{1,3}.\d{1,3}.\d{1,3}.\d{1,3})`

- Match the protocol: `((?<=[\d{1,3}\.\d{1,3}\.\d{1,3}\.\d{1,3}]\s))+\d{1,3}\.\d{1,3}\.\d{1,3}\.\d{1,3}`

Further reading on regular expressions can be found at Wikipedia:

`http://en.wikipedia.org/wiki/Regular_expression`

These extra fields can then be added to the fields or tags and used later for analysis or search and grouping.

 Drools also includes a module called **Drools Fusion** that essentially supports **Complex Event Processing** (**CEP**). It is often referred to as an emerging enterprise approach, which may be true, but practically it simply means that the rules engine understands temporal concerns. Using temporal operators, it can correlate events over time and derive new knowledge or trigger actions. These temporal operators are supported based on the bolt implementation in this recipe. For more information, browse to the following link:

`http://www.jboss.org/drools/drools-fusion.html`

Indexing and persisting the log data

Log data needs to be stored for some defined period of time in order to be useful; it also needs to be searchable. In order to achieve this, the recipe integrates with an open source product call **Elastic Search**, which is a general-use, clustered search engine with a RESTful API (`http://www.elasticsearch.org/`).

How to do it...

1. Create a new `BaseRichBolt` class called `IndexerBolt` and declare the `org.elasticsearch.client.Client` client as a private member variable. You must initialize it as follows within the `prepare` method:

```
if((Boolean)stormConf.get(backtype.storm.Config.TOPOLOGY_DEBUG) ==
true){
        node = NodeBuilder.nodeBuilder().local(true).node();
        } else {
            String clusterName = (String) stormConf.get(Conf.ELASTIC_
            CLUSTER_NAME);
```

```
        if(clusterName == null)
            clusterName = Conf.DEFAULT_ELASTIC_CLUSTER;
        node = NodeBuilder.nodeBuilder().
                clusterName(clusterName).node();
    }
    client = node.client();
```

2. The `LogEntry` object can then be indexed during the `execute` method of the bolt:

```
LogEntry entry = (LogEntry)input.getValueByField(FieldNames.LOG_
ENTRY);
    if(entry == null){
        LOG.fatal( "Received null or incorrect value from
                    tuple" );
        return;
    }
    String toBeIndexed = entry.toJSON().toJSONString();
    IndexResponse response = client.prepareIndex(INDEX_
NAME,INDEX_TYPE)
            .setSource(toBeIndexed)
            .execute().actionGet();
    if(response == null)
        LOG.error("Failed to index Tuple: " +
                input.toString());
    else{
        if(response.getId() == null)
            LOG.error("Failed to index Tuple: " +
                    input.toString());
        else{
            LOG.debug("Indexing success on Tuple: " +
                    input.toString());
            collector.emit(new Values(entry,response.getId()));
        }
    }
```

3. The unit test of this bolt is not obvious; it is therefore worthwhile to give some explanation here. Create a new JUnit 4 unit test in your test source folder under the `storm.cookbook.log` package. Add a private inner class called `StoringMatcher` as follows:

```
private static class StoringMatcher extends BaseMatcher<Values> {
        private final List<Values> objects = new
ArrayList<Values>();
        @Override
        public boolean matches(Object item) {
            if (item instanceof Values) {
                objects.add((Values) item);
```

```
      return true;
    }
    return false;
  }

  @Override
  public void describeTo(Description description) {
    description.appendText("any integer");
  }

  public Values getLastValue() {
    return objects.remove(0);
  }
 }
```

4. Then implement the actual test method as follows:

```
@Test
  public void testIndexing() throws IOException {
    //Config, ensure we are in debug mode
    Map config = new HashMap();
    config.put(backtype.storm.Config.TOPOLOGY_DEBUG, true);
        Node node = NodeBuilder.nodeBuilder()
                    .local(true).node();
        Client client = node.client();

        final OutputCollector collector =
                context.mock(OutputCollector.class);
        IndexerBolt bolt = new IndexerBolt();
        bolt.prepare(config, null, collector);

        final LogEntry entry = getEntry();

        final Tuple tuple = getTuple();
        final StoringMatcher matcher = new StoringMatcher();
        context.checking(new Expectations(){{
            oneOf(tuple).getValueByField(FieldNames.LOG_ENTRY);will
(returnValue(entry));
            oneOf(collector).emit(with(matcher));
        }});

        bolt.execute(tuple);
        context.assertIsSatisfied();

        //get the ID for the index
        String id = (String) matcher.getLastValue().get(1);
```

```
//Check that the indexing working
GetResponse response =
client.prepareGet(IndexerBolt.INDEX_NAME
,IndexerBolt.INDEX_TYPE,id)
        .execute()
        .actionGet();
assertTrue(response.exists());
}
```

How it works...

Elastic Search provides a complete client API for Java (given that it is implemented in Java), making integration with it quite trivial. The `prepare` method of the bolt will create a cluster node in either the local or clustered mode. The cluster mode will join an existing cluster based on the name provided with a local storage node being created on the current node; this prevents the double-hop latency of a write over a different transport.

 Elastic Search is a large complex system in its own right; it is recommended that you read the provided documentation in order to understand the operational and provisioning concerns.

When Storm is in the debug mode, the Elastic Search node will run an embedded cluster, with many nodes (if requested) being executed within the same JVM. This is obviously useful for unit testing purposes. This is all enabled in the `prepare` method of the bolt.

```
if((Boolean)stormConf.get(backtype.storm.Config.TOPOLOGY_DEBUG) ==
true){
        node = NodeBuilder.nodeBuilder().local(true).node();
    } else {
```

When a tuple is received, the `LogEntry` object is extracted and the JSON contents of `LogEntry` are sent to Elastic Search.

```
String toBeIndexed = entry.toJSON().toJSONString();
IndexResponse response =
        client.prepareIndex(INDEX_NAME,INDEX_TYPE)
    .setSource(toBeIndexed)
    .execute().actionGet();
```

The ID of the log within the Elastic Search cluster is then extracted from the response and emitted with the `LogEntry` objects to downstream bolts. In this particular recipe, we will only use this value for unit testing; however, downstream bolts could easily be added to persist this value against some log statistics that would be extremely useful within a user interface for drilldown purposes.

```
collector.emit(new Values(entry,response.getId()));
```

The unit test for this particular bolt is quite tricky. This is because, in a typical unit test, we know what the expected outcome is before we run the test. In this case, we don't know the ID until we have received the response from the Elastic Search cluster. This makes expressing expectations difficult, especially if we want to validate the log in the search engine. To achieve this, we make use of a custom matcher for JMock. The key method in the custom matcher is the `matches` method.

```
public boolean matches(Object item) {
        if (item instanceof Values) {
          objects.add((Values) item);
            return true;
        }
        return false;
    }
```

This method simply ensures that an instance of `Values` is returned but it also holds onto the value for later evaluation. This allows us to set the following set of expectations:

```
context.checking(new Expectations(){{
        oneOf(tuple).getValueByField(FieldNames
                .LOG_ENTRY);will(returnValue(entry));
        oneOf(collector).emit(with(matcher));
        }});
```

And then retrieve the record ID and validate it against the embedded Elastic Search cluster.

```
String id = (String) matcher.getLastValue().get(1);
GetResponse response = client.prepareGet(IndexerBolt
                .INDEX_NAME,IndexerBolt.INDEX_TYPE,id)
            .execute()
            .actionGet();
        assertTrue(response.exists());
```

If you would like to be able to search the logfiles in the cluster, download and install the excellent log search front engine, Kibana, from `kibana.org`. This recipe has maintained the JSON log structure from logstash and Kibana is designed as the frontend for logstash on Elastic Search; it will work seamlessly with this recipe. It also uses the Twitter Bootstrap GUI framework, meaning that you can integrate it with the analytics dashboard quite easily.

Counting and persisting log statistics

There are many statistics that can be gathered for log streams; for the purposes of this recipe and to illustrate the concept, only a single-time series will be dealt with (log volume per minute); however, this should fully illustrate the design and approach for implementing other analyses.

How to do it...

1. Download and install the `storm-cassandra contrib` project into your Maven repository:

```
git clone https://github.com/quintona/storm-cassandra
cd storm-cassandra
mvn clean install
```

2. Create a new `BaseRichBolt` class called `VolumeCountingBolt` in the `storm.cookbook.log` package. The bolt must declare three output fields:

```
public void declareOutputFields(OutputFieldsDeclarer declarer) {
        declarer.declare(new Fields(FIELD_ROW_KEY,
                        FIELD_COLUMN, FIELD_INCREMENT));
    }
```

3. Then implement a static utility method to derive the minute representation of the log's time:

```
public static Long getMinuteForTime(Date time) {
        Calendar c = Calendar.getInstance();
        c.setTime(time);
        c.set(Calendar.SECOND,0);
        c.set(Calendar.MILLISECOND, 0);
        return c.getTimeInMillis();
    }
```

4. Implement the `execute` method (yes, it is that short):

```
LogEntry entry = (LogEntry) input.getValueByField(FieldNames.LOG_
ENTRY);
        collector.emit(new Values(getMinuteForTime(entry.
getTimestamp()), entry.getSource(),1L));
```

5. Finally, create the `LogTopology` class as per the pattern presented in *Chapter 1, Setting Up Your Development Environment*, and create the topology as follows:

```
builder.setSpout("logSpout", new LogSpout(), 10);
builder.setBolt("logRules", new LogRulesBolt(), 10).
shuffleGrouping("logSpout");

builder.setBolt("indexer", new IndexerBolt(), 10).
shuffleGrouping("logRules");
builder.setBolt("counter", new VolumeCountingBolt(), 10).
shuffleGrouping("logRules");
CassandraCounterBatchingBolt logPersistenceBolt = new
    CassandraCounterBatchingBolt(
    Conf.COUNT_CF_NAME, VolumeCountingBolt.FIELD_ROW_KEY,
```

```
        VolumeCountingBolt.FIELD_INCREMENT );
          logPersistenceBolt.setAckStrategy
            (AckStrategy.ACK_ON_RECEIVE);
          builder.setBolt("countPersistor",
            logPersistenceBolt, 10).shuffleGrouping("counter");


    conf.put(Conf.REDIS_PORT_KEY, Conf.DEFAULT_JEDIS_PORT);
    conf.put(CassandraBolt.CASSANDRA_KEYSPACE, Conf.LOGGING_KEYSPACE);
```

How it works...

This implementation looks surprisingly simple, and it is. It makes use of the `storm-cassandra` project (a type of `storm-contrib`) to abstract all the persistence complexity away. The `storm-cassandra` project integrates Storm and Cassandra by providing a generic and configurable `backtype.storm.Bolt` implementation that writes the `StormTuple` objects to a Cassandra column family.

Cassandra is a column family database (`http://cassandra.apache.org/`). Cassandra's column family data model offers the convenience of column indexes with the performance of log-structured updates, strong support for materialized view, and powerful built-in caching. A recent addition to the Cassandra functionality is that of counter columns, which are essentially persistent columns, within a given column family, that can be incremented safely from anywhere in the cluster.

The `storm-cassandra` project provides two styles of persistence, firstly for standard Cassandra column families and secondly for counter-based columns. We will focus on the second type, as it is appropriate for our use case; you can read about the other style on the project's README file but it is essentially the same.

An instance of the `CassandraCounterBatchingBolt` class does all the work for us. It expects to be told which column family to use, which tuple field to use for the row key and which tuple field to use for the increment amount. It will then increment columns by that amount based on the remaining fields in the tuple.

Consider the following constructor:

```
CassandraCounterBatchingBolt logPersistenceBolt = new CassandraCounter
BatchingBolt("columnFamily", "RowKeyField", "IncrementAmountField" );
```

And the following tuple as input:

```
{rowKey: 12345, IncrementAmount: 1L, IncrementColumn: 'SomeCounter'}
```

This will increment the `SomeCounter` counter column by `1L` in the `columnFamily` column family.

A key mind shift for any developer with a relational database background is data modeling in a column family database. Column family databases, as part of the big data family of databases, promote the use of highly denormalized data models. This approach removes table relationships and their locking concerns and enables massive-scale parallel read and write processing on the database. This promotes data duplication; however, given the cost of commodity disks, this is seen as a small sacrifice in order to meet the scaling objectives of today. The mind shift is to think of data models in terms of the queries that we will perform on the dataset, rather than modeling real-world entities into concise normalized structures. The query we are trying to answer with this data model is essentially this: select all total count for all logfiles for a given point in time.

This approach allows us to easily derive this data by emitting a tuple to count that total; we can easily emit a tuple to answer any other question, and examples could include the following:

▶ What do my volume trends look like across any given time period, be it day, month, or year?

▶ What are the most popular stems within my logfiles?

 Column families can contain more than counts, design any denormalized structure, and emit a tuple to represent a set of columns for that row; if the row already exists, the columns will simply be added or updated. This can become extremely powerful.

Creating an integration test for the log stream cluster

Integration testing is obviously a vital task in the delivery process. There are many types of integration testing. Unit integration testing involves integration testing a topology, typically as part of the continuous integration build cycle, and should be seen as complementary to the necessary functional style of integration testing of a deployed cluster. The integration test presented here is essentially the same as that of the integration test presented in *Chapter 1, Setting Up Your Development Environment*; however, it is sufficiently complex to warrant an explanation here.

How to do it...

Start by creating the unit test.

1. Using Eclipse, create a JUnit 4 test case called `IntegrationTestTopology` under the unit testing source folder of your project in the `storm.cookbook.log` package. Add a `setup` method that should be invoked before the class:

```
@BeforeClass
    public static void setup() throws Exception {
```

```
        setupCassandra();
        setupElasticSearch();
        setupTopology();
    }
```

2. Then create each of the associated `setup` methods; first set up an embedded version of Cassandra:

```java
private static void setupCassandra() throws Exception {
        cassandra = new EmbeddedCassandra(9171);
        cassandra.start();
        //Allow some time for it to start
        Thread.sleep(3000);

        AstyanaxContext<Cluster> clusterContext = new
AstyanaxContext.Builder()
                .forCluster("ClusterName")
                .withAstyanaxConfiguration(
                    new AstyanaxConfigurationImpl()
                        .setDiscoveryType(NodeDiscoveryType.NONE))
                .withConnectionPoolConfiguration(
                    new ConnectionPoolConfigurationImpl("MyConnectio
nPool")
                        .setMaxConnsPerHost(1).setSeeds(
                            "localhost:9171"))
                .withConnectionPoolMonitor(new
CountingConnectionPoolMonitor())
                .buildCluster(ThriftFamilyFactory.getInstance());

        clusterContext.start();
        Cluster cluster = clusterContext.getEntity();
        KeyspaceDefinition ksDef = cluster.makeKeyspaceDefinition();

        Map<String, String> stratOptions = new HashMap<String,
String>();
        stratOptions.put("replication_factor", "1");
        ksDef.setName(Conf.LOGGING_KEYSPACE)
                .setStrategyClass("SimpleStrategy")
                .setStrategyOptions(stratOptions)
                .addColumnFamily(
                    cluster.makeColumnFamilyDefinition().
setName(Conf.COUNT_CF_NAME)
                        .setComparatorType("UTF8Type")
                        .setKeyValidationClass("UTF8Type")
                        .setDefaultValidationClass("CounterColumnT
ype"));
```

```
              cluster.addKeyspace(ksDef);


    }
```

3. Then set up a local, embedded instance of Elastic Search:

```
private static void setupElasticSearch() throws Exception {
        Node node = NodeBuilder.nodeBuilder().local(true).node();
        client = node.client();
        //allow time for the node to be available
        Thread.sleep(5000);
    }
```

4. Finally, set up the actual topology to be tested:

```
private static void setupTopology() {
        // We want all output tuples coming to the mock for
        // testing purposes
        topology.getBuilder().setBolt("testBolt", testBolt, 1)
              .globalGrouping("indexer");
        // run in local mode, but we will shut the cluster
        // down when we are finished
        topology.runLocal(0);
        // jedis required for input and output of the cluster
        jedis = new Jedis("localhost",
              Integer.parseInt(Conf.DEFAULT_JEDIS_PORT));
        jedis.connect();
        jedis.flushDB();
        // give it some time to startup before running the
        // tests.
        Utils.sleep(5000);
    }
```

5. This will set up the fixtures we require in order to test our topology; we also need to shut these down gracefully at the end of the test, so add the AfterClass method for the test suite:

```
@AfterClass
    public static void shutDown() {
        topology.shutDownLocal();
        jedis.disconnect();
        client.close();
        cassandra.stop();
    }
```

6. Finish off by implementing the actual test case:

```
@Test
    public void inputOutputClusterTest() throws Exception {
        String testData = UnitTestUtils.readFile("/testData1.json");
        jedis.rpush("log", testData);
        LogEntry entry = UnitTestUtils.getEntry();
        long minute = VolumeCountingBolt.getMinuteForTime(entry.
getTimestamp());
        Utils.sleep(6000);
        String id = jedis.rpop(REDIS_CHANNEL);
        assertNotNull(id);
        // Check that the indexing working
        GetResponse response = client
                .prepareGet(IndexerBolt.INDEX_NAME,
                    IndexerBolt.INDEX_TYPE, id).execute().actionGet();
        assertTrue(response.exists());
        // now check that count has been updated in cassandra
        AstyanaxContext<Keyspace> astyContext = new AstyanaxContext
                                                .Builder()
            .forCluster("ClusterName")
            .forKeyspace(Conf.LOGGING_KEYSPACE)
            .withAstyanaxConfiguration(
                new AstyanaxConfigurationImpl()
                    .setDiscoveryType(NodeDiscoveryType.NONE))
            .withConnectionPoolConfiguration(
                new ConnectionPoolConfigurationImpl(
                                            "MyConnectionPool")
                    .setMaxConnsPerHost(1).setSeeds(
                        "localhost:9171"))
            .withConnectionPoolMonitor(
                            new CountingConnectionPoolMonitor())
            .buildKeyspace(ThriftFamilyFactory.getInstance());
        astyContext.start();
        Keyspace ks = astyContext.getEntity();
        Column<String> result = ks.prepareQuery(
                new ColumnFamily<String, String>(
                    Conf.COUNT_CF_NAME, StringSerializer.get(),
                    StringSerializer.get()))
```

```
            .getKey(Long.toString(minute)).getColumn(entry.
getSource())
            .execute().getResult();
        assertEquals(1L, result.getLongValue());

    }
```

How it works...

This test case works by creating embedded instances of the required clusters for this topology, namely `Cassandra` and `Elastic Search`. As with the previous integration test, it then injects test data into the input channel and allows the log entry to flow through the topology, after which it validates the entry in the search engine and validates that the counter has incremented appropriately.

> This test will take longer to run than a standard unit test and therefore should not be included in your standard Maven build. The test should, however, be used as part of your local development workflow and validated further on a continuous integration server.

Creating a log analytics dashboard

The log analytics dashboard is a web application that presents aggregated data to the user, typically in a graphical manner. For achieving this, we must take cognizance of the following user interface design principles:

- **Laser focus**: This only shows what is required, creates a focal point based on what the user is trying to achieve, and doesn't detract from it with unnecessary clutter

- **Minimalistic**: This only incorporates required graphical features based on the usability concerns

- **Responsive**: This is a design approach that ensures that the display is clear and consistent regardless of the device it is viewed on, be it a PC or a tablet

- **Standards based**: This means that you shouldn't use any vendor-specific technologies that would preclude the viewing of the dashboard on devices such as the iPad

The dashboard in this recipe will present a single dynamic graph of the log volume by minute per logfile. The following screenshot illustrates the relative expanded view output:

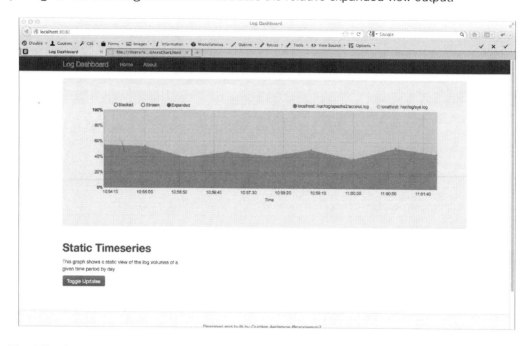

The following screenshot illustrates the detail inspection support output:

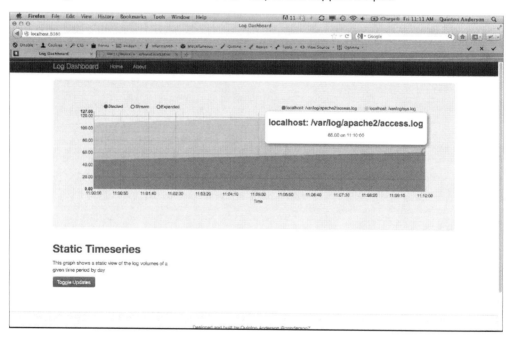

How to do it...

1. Create a new project called `log-web` using the standard Maven `archetype` command:

    mvn archetype:generate -DgroupId=storm.cookbook -DartifactId=log-web -DarchetypeArtifactId=maven-archetype-webapp

    This will generate a standard project structure and Maven POM file for you.

2. Open the `pom.xml` file and remove the default dependencies, replacing them with the following dependencies:

```
<dependency>
        <groupId>junit</groupId>
        <artifactId>junit</artifactId>
        <version>4.8.1</version>
        <scope>test</scope>
    </dependency>
    <dependency>
        <groupId>org.hectorclient</groupId>
        <artifactId>hector-core</artifactId>
        <version>1.1-2</version>
    </dependency>
    <dependency>
        <groupId>org.slf4j</groupId>
        <artifactId>slf4j-log4j12</artifactId>
        <version>1.6.1</version>
    </dependency>
    <dependency>
        <groupId>com.sun.jersey</groupId>
        <artifactId>jersey-server</artifactId>
        <version>1.16</version>
    </dependency>
    <dependency>
        <groupId>com.sun.jersey</groupId>
        <artifactId>jersey-grizzly2</artifactId>
        <version>1.16</version>
    </dependency>
    <dependency>
        <groupId>com.sun.jersey</groupId>
        <artifactId>jersey-servlet</artifactId>
        <version>1.16</version>
    </dependency>
    <dependency>
        <groupId>com.sun.jersey</groupId>
```

```
            <artifactId>jersey-json</artifactId>
            <version>1.16</version>
        </dependency>
        <dependency>
            <groupId>com.sun.jersey.contribs</groupId>
            <artifactId>jersey-multipart</artifactId>
            <version>1.16</version>
        </dependency>
        <dependency>
            <groupId>org.jmock</groupId>
            <artifactId>jmock-junit4</artifactId>
            <version>2.5.1</version>
            <scope>test</scope>
        </dependency>
        <dependency>
            <groupId>com.googlecode.json-simple</groupId>
            <artifactId>json-simple</artifactId>
            <version>1.1</version>
        </dependency>
```

3. Then add the following build plugins to the `build` section of the POM:

```
<plugins>
        <plugin>
            <groupId>org.mortbay.jetty</groupId>
            <artifactId>jetty-maven-plugin</artifactId>
        </plugin>
        <plugin>
            <groupId>org.codehaus.mojo</groupId>
            <artifactId>exec-maven-plugin</artifactId>
            <executions>
                <execution>
                    <goals>
                        <goal>java</goal>
                    </goals>
                </execution>
            </executions>
        </plugin>
        <plugin>
            <artifactId>maven-compiler-plugin</artifactId>
            <version>2.3</version>
            <configuration>
                <source>1.6</source>
                <target>1.6</target>
                <optimize>true</optimize>
```

```
            <showDeprecation>true</showDeprecation>
            <showWarnings>true</showWarnings>
        </configuration>
    </plugin>
    <plugin>
        <groupId>org.codehaus.mojo</groupId>
        <artifactId>cassandra-maven-plugin</artifactId>
    </plugin>
</plugins>
```

4. Then import the project into Eclipse using the `mvn eclipse:eclipse` command and the Eclipse project import process.

5. The excellent Twitter Bootstrap GUI library will be used in the creation of the user interface. Start by downloading this into a separate location on your drive and expanding it.

```
wget http://twitter.github.com/bootstrap/assets/bootstrap.zip

unzip boostrap.zip
```

6. The bootstrap gives us a rapid start by providing many practical examples; we will simply copy one and adapt it:

```
cp bootstrap/docs/examples/hero.html log-web/src/main/webapp/
index.html

cp bootstrap/docs/about log-web/src/main/webapp/about.html

cp bootstrap/docs/assets log-web/src/main/webapp/

cp boostrap/docs/assets log-web/src/main/webapp/

cp boostrap/docs/templates log-web/src/main/webapp/
```

 The Twitter Bootstrap is really quite an excellent departure point for any web-based GUI; it is highly recommended that you read the self-contained documentation in the downloaded package.

7. While there is much HTML to update, we will focus on the important elements: the central content and graph. Update the `index.html` file, replacing the existing `<div class="container">` tag and its contents with the following:

```
<div class="container">
    <div class="hero-unit">
        <div id="chart">
            <svg style="height: 300px;"></svg>
        </div>
    </div>
    <div class="row">
        <div class="span4">
```

```
<h2> Timeseries</h2>
<p>This graph shows a view of the log volumes
 of a given time period by day</p>
<button id="updateToggleButton" type="button"
class="btn btn-primary">Toggle Updates</button>
    </div>
  </div>
</div>
```

8. For the graph, we will use the excellent data-visualization library, D3 (http://d3js.org/), and some preconfigured models based on D3, called NVD3 (http://nvd3.org/), by adding their compiled JavaScript into our webapp's assets folder:

   wget https://github.com/novus/nvd3/zipball/master

   unzip novus-nvd3-4e12985.zip

   cp novus-nvd3-4e12985/nv.d3.js log-web/src/main/webapp/assets/js/

   cp novus-nvd3-4e12985/lib/d3.v2.js log-web/src/main/webapp/assets/js/

   cp novus-nvd3-4e12985/src/nv.d3.css log-web/src/main/webapp/assets/css/

9. Next, we include these into the HTML file and write the client-side JavaScript to retrieve the data and update the graph.

10. Add the following script includes at the bottom of the HTML file, after the other `<script>` tags:

    ```
    <script src="assets/js/d3.v2.js"></script>
    <script src="assets/js/nv.d3.js"></script>
    ```

11. And the CSS imports in the `html` header:

    ```
    <link type="text/css" rel="stylesheet" href="assets/css/nv.d3.css">
    ```

12. Then add our custom JavaScript into a `<script></script>` tag below the other script imports, towards the bottom of the file:

    ```
    var chart;
        var continueUpdates = true;
        nv.addGraph(function () {
            chart = nv.models.stackedAreaChart()
                    .x(function(d) { return d[0] })
                    .y(function(d) { return d[1] })
                    .clipEdge(true);

            chart.xAxis
                    .tickFormat(function(d) { return d3.time.
    format('%X')(new Date(d)) })
    ```

```
                    .axisLabel('Time')
                    .showMaxMin(false);

        chart.yAxis
                    .axisLabel('Volume')
                    .tickFormat(d3.format(',.2f'));

        d3.select('#chart svg')
                    .datum(getdata())
                    .transition().duration(500)
                    .call(chart);

        nv.utils.windowResize(chart.update);

        chart.dispatch.on('stateChange', function (e) {
            nv.log('New State:', JSON.stringify(e));
        });

        return chart;
    });

    function update() {
        fetch();
        if (continueUpdates)
            setTimeout(update, 60000);
    }

    update();

    $(document).ready(function () {
        $('#updateToggleButton').bind('click', function () {
            if (continueUpdates) {
                continueUpdates = false;
            } else {
                continueUpdates = true;
                update();
            }
        });

    });
```

13. And then add the code to fetch the data from the server:

```
    var alreadyFetched = {};

    function getUrl(){
        var today = new Date();
        today.setSeconds(0);
```

```
        today.setMilliseconds(0);
        var timestamp = today.valueOf();
        var dataurl = "http://localhost:8080/services/LogCount/
                    TotalsForMinute/" + timestamp + "/";
        return dataurl;
}

function fetch() {
    // find the URL in the link right next to us
    var dataurl = getUrl();

    // then fetch the data with jQuery
    function onDataReceived(series) {
        // append to the existing data
        for(var i = 0; i < series.length; i++){
            if(alreadyFetched[series[i].FileName] == null){
                alreadyFetched[series[i].FileName] = {
                    FileName: series[i].FileName,
                    values: [{
                        Minute: series[i].Minute,
                        Total: series[i].Total
                    }]
                };
            } else {
                alreadyFetched[series[i].FileName].values.push({
                    Minute: series[i].Minute,
                    Total: series[i].Total
                });
                if(alreadyFetched[series[i].FileName].values.
length > 30){
                    alreadyFetched[series[i].FileName].values.
pop();
                }
            }
        }

        //update the graph
        d3.select('#chart svg')
            .datum(getdata())
            .transition().duration(500)
            .call(chart);
    }

    function onError(request, status, error){
        console.log("Received Error from AJAX: " +
                    request.responseText);
```

```
        }

        $.ajax({
            url:dataurl,
            type:'GET',
            dataType:'json',
            crossDomain: true,
            xhrFields: {
                withCredentials: true
            },
            success:onDataReceived,
            error:onError
        });
    }

    function getdata(){
        var series = [];
        var keys = [];
        for (key in alreadyFetched) {
            keys.push(key);
        }
        for(var i = 0; i < keys.length; i++){
            var newValues = [];
            for(var j = 0; j < alreadyFetched[keys[i]].values.
length;j++){
                newValues.push([alreadyFetched[keys[i]].values[j].
Minute, alreadyFetched[keys[i]].values[j].Total]);
            }
            series.push({
                key:alreadyFetched[keys[i]].FileName,
                values:newValues
            });
        }
        return series;
    }
```

14. This completes the client-side part of the implementation. In order to expose the data to the client layer, we need to expose services to retrieve the data.

15. Start by creating a utility class called `CassandraUtils` in the `storm.cookbook.services.resources` package and add the following content:

```
public class CassandraUtils {

    public static Cluster cluster;
    public static Keyspace keyspace;
```

```
    protected static Properties properties;

    public static boolean initCassandra(){
        properties = new Properties();
         try {
          properties.load(Main.class
             .getResourceAsStream("/cassandra.properties"));
         } catch (IOException ioe) {
             ioe.printStackTrace();
         }
        cluster = HFactory.getOrCreateCluster(properties.
                    getProperty("cluster.name",
                    "DefaultCluster"), properties.getProperty
                    ("cluster.hosts", "127.0.0.1:9160"));
        ConfigurableConsistencyLevel ccl = new
                    ConfigurableConsistencyLevel();
        ccl.setDefaultReadConsistencyLevel
                    (HConsistencyLevel.ONE);

        String keyspaceName = properties.getProperty(
                    "logging.keyspace", "Logging");

        keyspace = HFactory.createKeyspace(
                    keyspaceName, cluster, ccl);

        return (cluster.describeKeyspace(
                    keyspaceName) != null);
    }

}
```

16. Then create the `LogCount` class in the same package, which essentially exposes a RESTful lookup service:

```
@Path("/LogCount")
public class LogCount {

    @GET
    @Path("/TotalsForMinute/{timestamp}")
    @Produces("application/json")
    public String getMinuteTotals(@PathParam("timestamp") String
timestamp){
        SliceCounterQuery<String, String> query =
            HFactory.createCounterSliceQuery(
                CassandraUtils.keyspace,
                StringSerializer.get(),
                StringSerializer.get());
```

```
query.setColumnFamily("LogVolumeByMinute");
query.setKey(timestamp);
query.setRange("", "", false, 100);

QueryResult<CounterSlice<String>> result = query.execute();

Iterator<HCounterColumn<String>> it =
        result.get().getColumns().iterator();
JSONArray content = new JSONArray();
while (it.hasNext()) {
    HCounterColumn<String> column = it.next();
    JSONObject fileObject = new JSONObject();
    fileObject.put("FileName", column.getName());
    fileObject.put("Total", column.getValue());
    fileObject.put("Minute", Long.parseLong(timestamp));
    content.add(fileObject);
}
return content.toJSONString();
    }
}
```

17. Finally, you expose the service by creating the `LogServices` class:

```
@ApplicationPath("/")
public class LogServices extends Application {

    public LogServices(){
        CassandraUtils.initCassandra();
    }
    @Override
    public Set<Class<?>> getClasses() {
      final Set<Class<?>> classes = new HashSet<Class<?>>();
      // register root resource
      classes.add(LogCount.class);
      return classes;
    }
}
```

18. Then configure the `web.xml` file:

```
<web-app>
  <display-name>Log-Web</display-name>
  <servlet>
    <servlet-name>
      storm.cookbook.services.LogServices</servlet-name>
    <servlet-class>
```

```
           com.sun.jersey.spi.container.servlet.ServletContainer
        </servlet-class>
        <init-param>
            <param-name>javax.ws.rs.Application</param-name>
                <param-value>
                   storm.cookbook.services.LogServices
                </param-value>
        </init-param>
        <load-on-startup>1</load-on-startup>
    </servlet>
    <servlet-mapping>
        <servlet-name>
        storm.cookbook.services.LogServices</servlet-name>
        <url-pattern>/services/*</url-pattern>
    </servlet-mapping>
</web-app>
```

19. You can now run your project using the following command from the root of your web-log project:

mvn jetty:run

Your dashboard will then be available at localhost:8080.

How it works...

At a high level, the dashboard works by periodically querying the server for counts for a given time. It maintains an in-memory structure on the client side to hold the results of these queries and then feeds the consolidated two-dimensional array into the graph class. Take a look at the HTML; the following code defines where the graph will be displayed:

```
<div id="chart">
    <svg style="height: 300px;"></svg>
</div>
```

The chart is defined by the following:

```
nv.addGraph(function () {
        chart = nv.models.stackedAreaChart()
                .x(function(d) { return d[0] })
                .y(function(d) { return d[1] })
                .clipEdge(true);

        chart.xAxis
                .tickFormat(function(d) { return
                    d3.time.format('%X')(new Date(d)) })
```

```
                .axisLabel('Time')
                .showMaxMin(false);

    chart.yAxis
                .axisLabel('Volume')
                .tickFormat(d3.format(',.2f'));

    d3.select('#chart svg')
                .datum(getdata())
                .transition().duration(500)
                .call(chart);

    nv.utils.windowResize(chart.update);


    chart.dispatch.on('stateChange', function (e) {
        nv.log('New State:', JSON.stringify(e));
    });

    return chart;
});
```

The in-memory structure is essentially simply a two-dimensional array of values and so it is important to map these onto the x and y axes on the graph, which is done through the following:

```
chart = nv.models.stackedAreaChart()
                .x(function(d) { return d[0] })
                .y(function(d) { return d[1] })
                .clipEdge(true);
```

Data is fetched through the `fetch()` method, which issues an Ajax asynchronus request to the server. Once the response is received, it is added to the in-memory structure in the `onDataReceived(series)` method. Finally, the `getdata()` method maps the log structure into a two-dimension array to be displayed by the graph.

On the server side, the service is exposed via **Jersey**. It is the open source, production-quality, JSR 311 Reference Implementation for building RESTful web services. Services are defined using annotations. For this recipe, only the single service is defined by the following annotations to the `LogCount` class:

```
@Path("/LogCount")
public class LogCount {

    @GET
    @Path("/TotalsForMinute/{timestamp}")
    @Produces("application/json")
    public String getMinuteTotals(@PathParam("timestamp") String
timestamp){
```

This service will then essentially be available from `localhost:8080/services/`
`LogCount/TotalForMinutes/[timestamp]`. The value passed into the `timestamp`
variable will be used in performing the lookup against Cassandra. The results of the query are
then mapped onto a JSON object and returned to the caller:

```
Iterator<HCounterColumn<String>> it = result.get().getColumns().
iterator();
        JSONArray content = new JSONArray();
        while (it.hasNext()) {
            HCounterColumn<String> column = it.next();
            JSONObject fileObject = new JSONObject();
            fileObject.put("FileName", column.getName());
            fileObject.put("Total", column.getValue());
            fileObject.put("Minute", Long.parseLong(timestamp));
            content.add(fileObject);
        }
        return content.toJSONString();
```

It is usually quite difficult to bring up the entire topology and set of clusters in
order to simply test the web application; a convenient `main` class is provided
in the supporting material that populates the column family with random
data, allowing for easy testing of the web application in isolation

3
Calculating Term Importance with Trident

In this chapter we will cover:

▸ Creating a URL stream using a Twitter filter

▸ Deriving a clean stream of terms from the documents

▸ Calculating the relative importance of each term

Introduction

This chapter will present the implementation of a very well-known data processing algorithm, **Term Frequency–Inverse Document Frequency** (**TF-IDF**), using Storm's Trident API. TF-IDF is a numerical statistic that reflects how important a word is to a document within a collection of documents. This is often a key concern in search engines but is also an important starting point in sentiment mining, as the trend of the important words within textual content can be an extremely useful predictor or an analytical tool.

> TF-IDF drives many search engines, such as Apache Lucence. If you want the details of how it is used in this context, please read the documentation for the `Similarity` class in Apache Lucence at `http://lucene.apache.org/core/2_9_4/api/all/org/apache/lucene/search/Similarity.html`.

According to the Storm project wiki (`https://github.com/nathanmarz/storm/wiki/Trident-tutorial`), Trident is a new high-level abstraction for doing real-time computing on top of Storm. It allows you to seamlessly intermix high throughput (millions of messages per second) and stateful stream processing with low-latency-distributed querying. If you're familiar with high-level batch processing tools such as **Pig** or **Cascading**, the concepts of Trident will be very familiar: Trident has joins, aggregations, grouping, functions, and filters. In addition to these, Trident adds primitives for doing stateful, incremental processing on top of any database or persistence store. Trident has consistent, exactly-once semantics; so it is easy to reason about Trident topologies.

Within the Big Data architecture, such as Lambda, Trident then becomes a key component providing the real-time portion of the data stream, which is then augmented with a historical batch of data to form a complete dataset. We will also see how DRPC easily enables such architecture in a later chapter. For some background on the Lambda architecture, please see this blog post at the following link:

`http://nathanmarz.com/blog/how-to-beat-the-cap-theorem.html`

Creating a URL stream using a Twitter filter

There are many approaches to sourcing input documents for the TF-IDF implementation. This recipe will present an approach using Twitter.

Twitter provides a stream API that allows you to receive a sample of the total tweets within Twitter. The approach of using a sample is more than sufficient for most applications, as more data may not improve your results, especially in any meaningful way relative to the costs involved. For this reason, this is the only way Twitter allows you to consume the data without special agreements in place.

Tweet status streams can be filtered using the Twitter streaming API, so that only a subset of the population is sampled and delivered in a stream. This enables one to listen for tweets for a particular topic. Furthermore, tweets often have links attached to them, which is where the bulk of the information is held given the small character limit on the tweet itself.

The approach for this recipe is therefore to subscribe to a Twitter stream using a filter and then extract the URLs contained within the tweets and emit them into the topology. These links will later be used to download the content of the documents to which they refer and calculate the TF-IDF value for each term within the document content.

How to do it...

Start by creating the project directory and standard Maven folder structure (`http://maven.apache.org/guides/introduction/introduction-to-the-standard-directory-layout.html`).

1. Create the POM as per the *Creating a "Hello World" topology* recipe in *Chapter 1, Setting Up Your Development Environment*, updating the `<artifactId>` and `<name>` tag values to `tfidf-topology`, and include the following dependencies:

`<groupId>`	`<artifactId>`	`<version>`	`<scope>`
`org.slf4j`	`slf4j-log4j12`	`1.6.1`	
`org.jmock`	`jmock-legacy`	`2.5.1`	`test`
`storm`	`storm`	`0.9.0-wip16`	`provided`
`org.twitter4j`	`twitter4j-core`	`[3.0,)`	
`org.twitter4j`	`twitter4j-stream`	`[3.0,)`	
`com.googlecode.json-simple`	`json-simple`	`1.1`	
`org.jmock`	`jmock-junit4`	`2.5.1`	`test`
`redis.clients`	`jedis`	`2.1.0`	
`org.apache.tika`	`tika-parsers`	`1.2`	
`org.apache.lucene`	`lucene-analyzers`	`3.6.2`	
`org.apache.lucene`	`lucene-spellchecker`	`3.6.2`	
`edu.washington.cs.knowitall`	`morpha-stemmer`	`1.0.4`	
`trident-cassandra`	`trident-cassandra`	`0.0.1-wip2`	

2. Import the project into Eclipse after generating the Eclipse project files:

```
mvn eclipse:eclipse
```

3. Create a new spout called `TwitterSpout` that extends from `BaseRichSpout`, and add the following member-level variables:

```
LinkedBlockingQueue<Status> queue = null;
    TwitterStream twitterStream;
    String[] trackTerms;
    long maxQueueDepth;
    SpoutOutputCollector collector;
```

4. In the `open` method of the spout, initialize the blocking queue and create a Twitter stream listener:

```
queue = new LinkedBlockingQueue<Status>(1000);
    StatusListener listener = new StatusListener()
{

        @Override
          public void onStatus(Status status) {
             if(queue.size() < maxQueueDepth){
               LOG.trace("TWEET Received: " + status);
               queue.offer(status);
            } else {
             LOG.error("Queue is now full, the following
                      message is dropped: "+status);

        }
      }
```

5. Then create the Twitter stream and filter, as follows:

```
twitterStream = new TwitterStreamFactory().getInstance();
        twitterStream.addListener(listener);
        FilterQuery filter = new FilterQuery();
        filter.count(0);
        filter.track(trackTerms);
        twitterStream.filter(filter);
```

6. You then need to emit the tweet into the topology.

```
public void nextTuple() {
    Status ret = queue.poll();
    if(ret == null){
      try { Thread.sleep(50); }
      catch (InterruptedException e) {}
    } else {
      collector.emit(new Values(ret));
    }

  }
```

7. Next, you must create a bolt to publish the tuple persistently to another topology within the same cluster. Create a `BaseRichBolt` class called `PublishURLBolt` that doesn't declare any fields, and provide the following `execute` method:

```
public void execute(Tuple input) {
    Status ret = (Status) input.getValue(0);
    URLEntity[] urls = ret.getURLEntities();
    for(int i = 0; i < urls.length;i++){
      jedis.rpush("url", urls[i].getURL().trim());
    }

  }
```

8. Finally, you will need to read the URL into a stream in the Trident topology. To do this, create another spout called `TweetURLSpout`:

```
@Override
public void declareOutputFields(OutputFieldsDeclarer
                    outputFieldsDeclarer) {
    outputFieldsDeclarer.declare(new Fields("url"));
}

@Override
public void open(Map conf, TopologyContext
  topologyContext, SpoutOutputCollector
  spoutOutputCollector) {
    host = conf.get(Conf.REDIS_HOST_KEY).toString();
    port = Integer.valueOf(conf.get(Conf
            .REDIS_PORT_KEY).toString());
    this.collector = spoutOutputCollector;
    connectToRedis();
}

private void connectToRedis() {
    jedis = new Jedis(host, port);
}

@Override
public void nextTuple() {
    String url = jedis.rpop("url");
    if(url==null) {
        try { Thread.sleep(50); }
        catch (InterruptedException e) {}
    } else {
        collector.emit(new Values(url));
    }
}
```

How it works...

The cluster will execute two separate topologies. The first topology will simply receive data from the Twitter API and publish it to a queue; the other topology will be the actual Trident topology that does all the heavy lifting. This separation by persistent queue is not only important from a best-practice perspective, but it also ensures that the production and consumption of data are completely decoupled. These are important reasons from the maintenance and stability perspective; the direct functional reason for the separation is the ability to implement exactly-once semantics that require a transactional spout, which we will cover in a later chapter.

The Twitter stream is received by using the Twitter4J library (`http://twitter4j.org/`) that takes care of everything for you, including listening appropriately for raw data from Twitter. An event listener must be provided to it in order to handle newly received tweets from the API. Because the listening process is executed in a separate thread, the listener posts them to a thread-safe queue:

```
queue.offer(status);
```

The tweet is then removed from the queue as part of the `nextTuple()` method of the spout and emitted into the topology:

```
Status ret = queue.poll();
```

The creation of the Twitter filter is the key for this approach. We are trying to discover the most important terms for a given topic; therefore, we need to set up an appropriate filter so that we only receive relevant tweets, as far as possible. The Twitter API documents the filter usage in great detail and it is important to understand this in order to construct an appropriate filter; this is available at the following link:

`https://dev.twitter.com/docs/streaming-apis/parameters#track`

The Twitter API is exposed via Twitter4J in the following calls within the `open` method:

```
FilterQuery filter = new FilterQuery();
        filter.count(0);
        filter.track(trackTerms);
        twitterStream.filter(filter);
```

> There are lock-free mechanisms to achieve the coordination between these threads. If your performance requirements call for it, take a look at the disruptor as an alternative for you (`http://lmax-exchange.github.com/disruptor/`).

There's more...

Testing the topology against an active Twitter stream is quite difficult because of the rate of unknown data being used as part of debugging and testing processes. It is therefore important to have a testing spout to inject URLs into the Trident topology. The Trident API ships with a testing utility to achieve this. Simply provide this spout to the Trident stream as an input parameter as opposed to `TweetURLSpout`:

```
FixedBatchSpout testSpout = new FixedBatchSpout(
        new Fields("url"), 1,
        new Values("http://t.co/hP5PM6fm"),
        new Values("http://t.co/xSFteG23"));
        testSpout.setCycle(true);
```

This will essentially inject a known set of URLs into the topology in a cycle, giving us a stable, predictable testing environment. This can be removed when we deploy to an actual cluster.

Finally, while you can use your username and password to access Twitter, this isn't advised. Rather, you should register your application by following the Twitter dev guides at `https://dev.twitter.com/docs`. Once you have done this, create a properties file within your `resources` folder with the following content:

```
oauth.consumerKey=XXX
oauth.consumerSecret=XXX
oauth.accessToken=XXXX
oauth.accessTokenSecret=XXXX
```

Deriving a clean stream of terms from the documents

This recipe consumes the URL stream, downloading the document content and deriving a clean stream of terms that are suitable for later analysis. A **clean term** is defined as a word that:

- ▶ Is not a stop word
- ▶ Is a valid dictionary word
- ▶ Is not a number or URL
- ▶ Is a lemma

A **lemma** is the canonical form of a word; for example, run, runs, ran, and running are forms of the same lexeme with "run" as the lemma. Lexeme, in this context, refers to the set of all the forms that have the same meaning, and lemma refers to the particular form that is chosen by convention to represent the lexeme.

The lemma is important for this recipe because it enables us to group terms that have the same meaning. Where their frequency of occurrence is important, this grouping is important.

 A lemma is similar to a stem; however, a stem is often not a valid dictionary word because it is derived algorithmically. Therefore, a lemma is preferred for this recipe, given that the imperative is "understanding" and not "searching" the order.

How to do it...

First we need to fetch the document content based on the URL:

1. Create a class named `DocumentFetchFunction`, that extends from `storm.trident.operation.BaseFunction`, and provide the following implementation for the `execute` method:

```
String url = tuple.getStringByField("url");
    try {
        Parser parser = new AutoDetectParser();
        Metadata metadata = new Metadata();
        ParseContext parseContext = new ParseContext();
        URL urlObject = new URL(url);
        ContentHandler handler = new BodyContentHandler(10 *
                                1024 * 1024);
        parser.parse((InputStream) urlObject.getContent(),
                    handler, metadata, parseContext);
        String[] mimeDetails = metadata.get("Content-Type")
                                    .split(";");
        if ((mimeDetails.length > 0)
            && (mimeTypes.contains(mimeDetails[0]))) {
          collector.emit(new Values(handler.toString(),
                        url.trim(), "twitter"));
        }
    } catch (Exception e) {
    }
```

2. Next we need to tokenize the document, create another class that extends from `BaseFunction` and call it `DocumentTokenizer`. Provide the following `execute` implementation:

```
String documentContents = tuple.getStringByField(TfidfTopologyFiel
ds.DOCUMENT);
    TokenStream ts = null;
    try {
        ts = new StopFilter( Version.LUCENE_30,
                    new StandardTokenizer(Version.LUCENE_30,
                    new StringReader(documentContents)),
                    StopAnalyzer.ENGLISH_STOP_WORDS_SET
            );
        CharTermAttribute termAtt =
                ts.getAttribute(CharTermAttribute.class);
            while(ts.incrementToken()) {
              String lemma = MorphaStemmer.stemToken(
                        termAtt.toString());
              lemma = lemma.trim().replaceAll("\n","")
```

```
                    .replaceAll("\r", "");
          collector.emit(new Values(lemma));
        }
    ts.close();
  } catch (IOException e) {
          LOG.error(e.toString());
  }
  finally {
    if(ts != null){
      try {
        ts.close();
      } catch (IOException e) {}
    }

  }
```

3. We then need to filter out all the invalid terms that may be emitted by this function. To do this, we need to implement another class that extends `BaseFunction` called `TermFilter`. The `execute` method of this function will simply call a checking function to optionally emit the received tuple. The checking function `isKeep()` should perform the following validations:

```
if(stem == null)
      return false;
  if(stem.equals(""))
    return false;
  if(filterTerms.contains(stem))
    return false;
  //we don't want integers
  try{
    Integer.parseInt(stem);
    return false;
  }catch(Exception e){}
  //or floating point numbers
  try{
    Double.parseDouble(stem);
    return false;
  }catch(Exception e){}
  try {
    return spellchecker.exist(stem);
  } catch (Exception e) {
    LOG.error(e.toString());
    return false;
  }
```

4. The dictionary needs to be initialized during the `prepare` method for this function:

```
public void prepare(Map conf, TridentOperationContext context){
    super.prepare(conf, context);
    File dir = new File(System.getProperty("user.home") +
            "/dictionaries");
    Directory directory;
    try {
        directory = FSDirectory.open(dir);
        spellchecker = new SpellChecker(directory);
        StandardAnalyzer analyzer = new
            StandardAnalyzer(Version.LUCENE_36);
        IndexWriterConfig config = new
            IndexWriterConfig(Version.LUCENE_36, analyzer);
        URL dictionaryFile = TermFilter.class.getResource("
            /dictionaries/fulldictionary00.txt");
        spellchecker.indexDictionary(new
            PlainTextDictionary(new File(
            dictionaryFile.toURI())), config, true);
    } catch (Exception e) {
        LOG.error(e.toString());
        throw new RuntimeException(e);
    }
}
```

5. Download the dictionary file from `http://dl.dropbox.com/u/7215751/JavaCodeGeeks/LuceneSuggestionsTutorial/fulldictionary00.zip` and place it in the `src/main/resources/dictionaries` folder of your project structure.

6. Finally, you need to create the actual topology, or at least partially for the moment. Create a class named `TermTopology` that provides a `main(String[] args)` method and creates a local mode cluster:

```
Config conf = new Config();
    conf.setMaxSpoutPending(20);
    conf.put(Conf.REDIS_HOST_KEY, "localhost");
    conf.put(Conf.REDIS_PORT_KEY, Conf.DEFAULT_JEDIS_PORT);

    if (args.length == 0) {
        LocalDRPC drpc = new LocalDRPC();
        LocalCluster cluster = new LocalCluster();
        cluster.submitTopology("tfidf", conf,
                            buildTopology(drpc));
        Thread.sleep(60000);
    }
```

7. Then build the appropriate portion of the topology:

```
public static StormTopology buildTopology(LocalDRPC drpc) {
    TridentTopology topology = new TridentTopology();
```

```
FixedBatchSpout testSpout = new FixedBatchSpout(
    new Fields("url"), 1,
    new Values("http://t.co/hP5PM6fm"),
    new Values("http://t.co/xSFteG23"));
testSpout.setCycle(true);

Stream documentStream = topology
    .newStream("tweetSpout", testSpout)
    .parallelismHint(20)
    .each(new Fields("url"),
    new DocumentFetchFunction(mimeTypes),
    new Fields("document", "documentId", "source"));

Stream termStream = documentStream
    .parallelismHint(20).each(new Fields("document"),
    new DocumentTokenizer(), new Fields("dirtyTerm"))
    .each(new Fields("dirtyTerm"), new TermFilter(),
    new Fields("term")).project(new
    Fields("term","documentId","source"));
```

How it works...

Trident's API provides for various types of operations. Functions are partition-local in nature, meaning that they are applied to each batch independently. A function takes in a set of input fields and emits zero or more tuples as output. The fields of the output tuple are appended to the original input tuple in the stream. If a function emits no tuples, the original input tuple is filtered out. Otherwise, the input tuple is duplicated for each output tuple.

The document fetch function takes a URL as input, fetches the document, and emits the document content, meaning that the resulting tuple will contain both the document content and the URL. If there are any problems fetching the document, it won't emit anything, thus acting as a natural filter.

The fetch function makes use of the Apache Tika library (http://tika.apache.org/) to fetch and extract the contents of the document:

```
Parser parser = new AutoDetectParser();
    Metadata metadata = new Metadata();
    ParseContext parseContext = new ParseContext();
    URL urlObject = new URL(url);
    ContentHandler handler = new BodyContentHandler(10 * 1024 *
        1024);
    parser.parse((InputStream) urlObject.getContent(), handler,
        metadata, parseContext);
```

And it then filters based on MIME type to ensure we only get the document types that we are looking for:

```
String[] mimeDetails = metadata.get("Content-Type").split(";");
    if ((mimeDetails.length > 0)
        && (mimeTypes.contains(mimeDetails[0]))) {
      collector.emit(new Values(handler.toString(), url.trim(),
                    "twitter"));
    }
```

The tokenize function does a little bit more than purely tokenizing the document. It makes use of the Apache Lucene's analyzer library (http://lucene.apache.org/) to tokenize and filter out the stop words as it proceeds further:

```
ts = new StopFilter(
        Version.LUCENE_30,
          new StandardTokenizer(Version.LUCENE_30, new
          StringReader(documentContents)),
          StopAnalyzer.ENGLISH_STOP_WORDS_SET
    );
```

It then makes use of the Morpha Stemmer library (http://www.informatics.sussex.ac.uk/research/groups/nlp/carroll/morph.html) to derive the word stem, or rather lemma, of each term. These values are then emitted as follows:

```
CharTermAttribute termAtt = ts.getAttribute(CharTermAttribute.class);
  while(ts.incrementToken()) {
    String lemma = MorphaStemmer.stemToken(termAtt.toString());
    lemma = lemma.trim().replaceAll("\n", "").replaceAll("\r", "")
        collector.emit(new Values(lemma));
    }
```

The `document` filter doesn't simply emit tuples that don't meet a set of criteria; among them is a dictionary lookup.

Importantly, the Trident API starts by defining a stream on the topology and linking in the document fetch function through the `each` function:

```
Stream documentStream = topology
        .newStream("tweetSpout", testSpout)
        .parallelismHint(20)
        .each(new Fields("url"),
            new DocumentFetchFunction(mimeTypes),
            new Fields("document", "documentId", "source"));
```

It then defines a `term` stream that tokenizes the documents on the `document` stream, filters the terms, and projects out the required fields:

```
Stream termStream = documentStream
        .parallelismHint(20)
        .each(new Fields("document"), new DocumentTokenizer(),
            new Fields("dirtyTerm"))
        .each(new Fields("dirtyTerm"), new TermFilter(),
            new Fields("term"))
        .project(new Fields("term","documentId","source"));
```

The projection essentially drops the fields from the tuples that aren't listed. This is important because we don't want to send the document content redundantly and unnecessarily around the network.

Calculating the relative importance of each term

The true power of Trident is demonstrated in this recipe, with many of the abstractions used in order to calculate the TF-IDF value. Before the recipe is presented, it is important to understand the simple math behind TF-IDF. We will need the following components to calculate the TF-IDF:

- ▸ `tf(t,d)`: This component specifies the term frequency, that is, the number of times a given term (`t`) appears in a given document (`d`)

- ▸ `df(t)`: This component specifies the document frequency, that is, how frequently a given term (`t`) appears across all documents

- ▸ `D`: This component specifies the document count, that is, the total number of documents

There are many ways to calculate the term frequency; for this recipe, we will use the raw frequency, that is, the number of times a term appears in the document. Based on this assumption, the formula for TF-IDF is:

$$tf(t,d) * \log \frac{D}{1 + df(t)}$$

How to do it...

1. Add the following API calls to the topology definition in the `TermTopology` class:

```
TridentState dfState = termStream.groupBy(
    new Fields("term")).persistentAggregate(
    getStateFactory("df"),
    new Count(), new Fields("df"));


TridentState dState = termStream.groupBy(
    new Fields("source")).persistentAggregate(
    getStateFactory("d"), new Count(),
    new Fields("d"));

topology.newDRPCStream("dQuery",drpc)
    .each(new Fields("args"), new Split(),
    new Fields("source")).stateQuery(dState,
    new Fields("source"), new MapGet(),
    new Fields("d_term", "currentD"));

topology.newDRPCStream("dfQuery",drpc)
    .each(new Fields("args"), new Split(),
    new Fields("term")).stateQuery(dfState,
    new Fields("term"), new MapGet(),
    new Fields("currentDf"));

Stream tfidfStream = termStream.groupBy(
    new Fields("documentId", "term"))
    .aggregate(new Count(), new Fields("tf"))
    .each(new Fields("term","documentId", "tf"),
    new TfidfExpression(), new Fields("tfidf"));
```

2. And then implement the `TfidfExpression` class by extending the `BaseFunction` interface and providing the `execute` method:

```
try {
    String result = execute("dQuery", "twitter");
    double d = Double.parseDouble(result);
    result = execute("dfQuery",
            tuple.getStringByField("term"));
    double df = Double.parseDouble(result);
    double tf = (double) tuple.getLongByField("tf");
    double tfidf = tf * Math.log(d / (1.0 + df));
    LOG.debug("Emitting new TFIDF(term,Document): ("
        + tuple.getStringByField("term") + ","
```

```
               + tuple.getStringByField("documentId") + ") = " +
                   tfidf);
       collector.emit(new Values(tfidf));
   } catch (Exception e) {
     LOG.error(e);
   }
}
```

How it works...

It is important at this point to understand the flow of data across the entire topology, as illustrated by the following diagram:

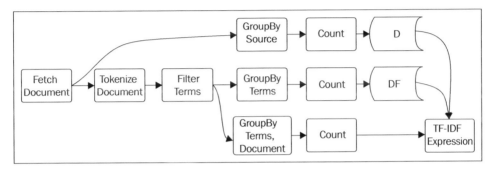

The initial data flow is that of a single stream; however, after the terms have been filtered, it branches off into three separate flows. Both D and df(t) are functions that are calculated across batches and over time, they are in a sense long-living concerns, while tf(t,d) is only applicable for the given batch.

The value for D is derived by grouping documents by some static property. In this case, the concept of source was introduced and, for the purposes of this recipe, will only have the value twitter. This property is important so that we can use a grouping around the state, which will allow us to easily re-use the map state that ships with Trident without having to define some custom state implementation. These API calls will effectively group around the static property and count all the documents:

```
TridentState dState = documentStream.groupBy(new Fields("source"))
        .persistentAggregate(getStateFactory("d"), new Count(), new
Fields("d"));
```

The same logic is applied to df(t), except that we group around the term. For both D and df(t), we make use of the persistentAggregate method and a map state, Cassandra in this case, to ensure that we maintain the state across batch boundaries.

Finally, we group and aggregate around the term and document to get the term frequency, which is a nonpersistent aggregate. The terms document ID and frequency are then passed to the expression that does a lookup of the other values using a DRPC query:

```
private String execute(String function, String args) throws
TException, DRPCExecutionException{
    if(client != null)
        return client.execute(function, args);
}
```

The queries are defined within the topology and simply executed, as shown in the preceding code snippet:

```
topology.newDRPCStream("dQuery",drpc)
        .each(new Fields("args"),
        new Split(), new Fields("source"))
        .stateQuery(dState, new Fields("source"), new MapGet(),
        new Fields("d_term", "currentD"));

topology.newDRPCStream("dfQuery",drpc)
        .each(new Fields("args"), new Split(),
        new Fields("term")).stateQuery(dfState,
        new Fields("term"), new MapGet(), new
        Fields("currentDf"));
```

Each query takes a set of arguments and passes them as a key to the MapGet query function. This simply does a lookup against a key and in our case will only ever return a single result because of the groupings applied before each persistentAggregate.

There's more...

It is important to have the schema defined correctly before executing your topology; this can be achieved by creating a text file called dropAndCreateSchema.txt with the following content:

```
drop keyspace trident_test;
create keyspace trident_test
    with strategy_options = [{replication_factor:1}]
    and placement_strategy =
                'org.apache.cassandra.locator.SimpleStrategy';

use trident_test;
create column family tfid
    with comparator = AsciiType
    and default_validation_class = 'UTF8Type'
    and key_validation_class = 'UTF8Type';
```

You can then apply this schema by executing the following command:

```
cassandra-cli --host localhost < dropAndCreateSchema.txt
```

4
Distributed Remote Procedure Calls

In this chapter we will cover:

- ▶ Using DRPC to complete the required processing
- ▶ Integration testing of a Trident topology
- ▶ Implementing a rolling window topology
- ▶ Simulating time in integration testing

Introduction

This chapter builds on the concepts introduced in *Chapter 3, Calculating Term Importance with Trident*, by providing the next steps towards a fully fledged enterprise-ready TF-IDF implementation. In this chapter we will investigate the usage of **distributed remote procedure calls** (**DRPC**) to complete a portion of the required processing in order to give us a point-in-time view of the TF-IDF value for a given term and document, as *Chapter 3, Calculating Term Importance with Trident*, focused on a purely streamed delivery of the TF-IDF values. We will then explore the usefulness of DRPC in terms of integration testing of a Trident topology. Trident has many useful stateful abstractions that we will need to properly exercise in our integration testing. Finally we will implement a rolling window addition to the TF-IDF algorithm, which will allow us to position our topology as a speed layer for a larger Lambda architecture.

A theoretical basis for DRPC and Trident API is required for this chapter; please take some time to read the Storm project documentation on these topics at the following links:

- ▶ https://github.com/nathanmarz/storm/wiki/Distributed-RPC
- ▶ https://github.com/nathanmarz/storm/wiki/Trident-API-Overview
- ▶ https://github.com/nathanmarz/storm/wiki/Trident-state

Lambda architecture is a term coined by *Nathan Marz*; it was first introduced in his blog entry on *How to beat the CAP theorem*. It provides an elegant combination of both batch and real-time data systems that are scalable and truly fault-tolerant.

A full understanding of the theoretical basis and approach is recommended; it is available at the following link:

```
http://nathanmarz.com/blog/how-to-beat-the-cap-
theorem.html
```

Using DRPC to complete the required processing

A classic design consideration within data systems is choosing an appropriate balance between precomputation and on-the-fly computation. Precomputation is often preferable; however, it isn't always possible. Either because the amount of potential data is far too large in practical terms, or because the final result is dependent on a point-in-time perspective of the data that is not possible to precompute.

In the previous chapter, we emitted a constant stream of TF-IDF values based on the documents received from Twitter and the Internet. The TF-IDF value is perfectly correct at the time when it is emitted; however, as time passes the value that was emitted is potentially invalidated because it is coupled to a global state that is affected by new tuples that arrive after the value was computed. In some applications this is the desired result; however, in other applications we need to know what the current value is at this point in time, not at some previous point in time. In this case, we need to compute as much state as is possible as a part of normal stream processing, and defer the remaining computation until the time of the query. This is a use case for which DRPC is ideally suited.

Trident provides a rich set of abstractions for querying sources of state and processing the resulting tuples using the same power that is inherent in any stream processing. Our ability to defer portions of the processing to a later time enables us to deal with use cases where state is only valid in the context of "now".

How to do it...

1. Create a new branch of your source using the following command:

    ```
    git branch chap4
    git checkout chap4
    ```

2. Create a new class named `SplitAndProjectToFields`, which extends from `BaseFunction`:

```
public void execute(TridentTuple tuple, TridentCollector
collector) {
    Values vals = new Values();
    for(String word: tuple.getString(0).split(" ")) {
            if(word.length() > 0) {
              vals.add(word);
            }
        }
    collector.emit(vals);

}
```

3. Once this is complete, edit the `TermTopology` class, and add the following method:

```
private static void addTFIDFQueryStream(TridentState
  tfState, TridentState dfState,
  TridentState dState, TridentTopology topology,
  LocalDRPC drpc) {
    topology.newDRPCStream("tfidfQuery",drpc)
        .each(new Fields("args"),
         new SplitAndProjectToFields(),
         new Fields("documentId", "term"))

        .each(new Fields(), new StaticSourceFunction(),
         new Fields("source")).stateQuery(tfState,
         new Fields("documentId", "term"),
         new MapGet(), new Fields("tf"))

        .stateQuery(dfState,new Fields("term"),
         new MapGet(), new Fields("df"))
        .stateQuery(dState,new Fields("source"),
         new MapGet(), new Fields("d"))

        .each(new Fields("term","documentId","tf","d","df"),
         new TfidfExpression(), new Fields("tfidf"))
        .each(new Fields("tfidf"), new FilterNull())
        .project(new Fields("documentId","term","tfidf"));
    }
```

4. Then update your `buildTopology` method by removing the final stream definition and adding the DRPC creation:

```
public static TridentTopology buildTopology(ITridentSpout spout,
LocalDRPC drpc) {
    TridentTopology topology = new TridentTopology();

    Stream documentStream = getUrlStream(topology, spout)
        .each(new Fields("url"),
        new DocumentFetchFunction(mimeTypes),
        new Fields("document", "documentId", "source"));

    Stream termStream = documentStream
        .parallelismHint(20)each(new Fields("document"),
        new DocumentTokenizer(), new Fields("dirtyTerm"))
        .each(new Fields("dirtyTerm"), new TermFilter(),
        new Fields("term"))
        .project(new Fields("term","documentId","source"));

    TridentState dfState = termStream.groupBy(
        new Fields("term")).persistentAggregate
        (getStateFactory("df"), new Count(),
        new Fields("df"));

    TridentState dState = documentStream.groupBy(
        new Fields("source")).persistentAggregate(
        getStateFactory("d"), new Count(), new Fields("d"));

    TridentState tfState = termStream.groupBy(
        new Fields("documentId", "term"))
        .persistentAggregate(getStateFactory("tf"),
        new Count(), new Fields("tf"));

    addTFIDFQueryStream(tfState, dfState, dState, topology,
                        drpc);

    return topology;
}
```

How it works...

At a high level, all we are doing as part of the stream processing is persisting computed values for `d`, `df (term)`, and `tf (document,term)`, but we don't calculate the final TF-IDF value. We defer this calculation until the time the value is requested.

The states are computed by the following Trident calls:

```
TridentState dfState = termStream.groupBy(new Fields("term"))
        .persistentAggregate(getStateFactory("df"), new Count(),
        new Fields("df"));

TridentState dState = documentStream.groupBy(
        new Fields("source")) .persistentAggregate(
        getStateFactory("d"), new Count(), new Fields("d"));

TridentState tfState = termStream.groupBy(
        new Fields("documentId", "term")).persistentAggregate(
        getStateFactory("tf"), new Count(), new Fields("tf"));
```

It is important to note the `GroupBy` definitions for each case. The d value is grouped by a static value for the source of the stream, which gives us a global count across batch boundaries.

The df value is grouped by the term, which will effectively give us a count of the number of documents that contain the term, again across batch boundaries.

Finally, the tf value is stored by the document and term that gives us a count of the term on a per document basis.

With these elements calculated, we can defer the calculation to a later point in time. This is enabled through DRPC:

```
private static void addTFIDFQueryStream(TridentState tfState,
        TridentState dfState,
        TridentState dState,
        TridentTopology topology, LocalDRPC drpc) {
    topology.newDRPCStream("tfidfQuery",drpc)
        .each(new Fields("args"), new SplitAndProjectToFields(),
            new Fields("documentId", "term"))
        .each(new Fields(), new StaticSourceFunction(),
            new Fields("source"))
        .stateQuery(tfState, new Fields("documentId", "term"),
            new MapGet(), new Fields("tf"))
        .stateQuery(dfState,new Fields("term"),
            new MapGet(), new Fields("df"))
        .stateQuery(dState,new Fields("source"),
            new MapGet(), new Fields("d"))
        .each(new Fields("term","documentId","tf","d","df"),
            new TfidfExpression(), new Fields("tfidf"))
        .each(new Fields("tfidf"), new FilterNull())
        .project(new Fields("documentId","term","tfidf"));
}
```

Let's just unpack that a bit. The first function splits out the arguments that will be passed to the DRPC call from a client.

```
.each(new Fields("args"), new SplitAndProjectToFields(), new
Fields("documentId", "term"))
```

The arguments will be passed to the DRPC call in the form `drpc.execute("tfidfQuery", "doc01 area")`. The arguments, `doc01` and `area`, should then be placed into a single tuple in the fields `documentId` and `term`. In order to achieve this, we can't simply apply a split function to the arguments, as this would generate many tuples. Instead we use the `SplitAndProjectToFields` function that we defined earlier:

```
public void execute(TridentTuple tuple, TridentCollector collector) {
    Values vals = new Values();
    for(String word: tuple.getString(0).split(" ")) {
        if(word.length() > 0) {
            vals.add(word);
        }
    }
    collector.emit(vals);

}
```

This function splits the input text based on " " (space) and then projects the values out to consecutive fields within the same tuple. Next we use a state query to add the value for `tf` to the tuple, based on values that were passed as arguments:

```
.stateQuery(tfState, new Fields("documentId", "term"), new MapGet(),
new Fields("tf"))
```

After this query is complete, the tuple would contain three fields: `documentId`, `term`, and `tf`, where `tf` is the value that we computed earlier.

Next we look up the value for `df`:

```
.stateQuery(dfState,new Fields("term"), new MapGet(), new
Fields("df"))
```

After this query is complete, the tuple will also contain a field for `df`. Finally we look up the value for `d` and add it to the tuple:

```
.stateQuery(dState,new Fields("source"), new MapGet(), new
Fields("d"))
```

Then we pass all the fields to the expression function that we created in *Chapter 3,
Calculating Term Importance with Trident*, and project just the final fields:

```
Fields("term","documentId","tf","d","df"), new TfidfExpression(), new
Fields("tfidf"))
        .each(new Fields("tfidf"), new FilterNull())
        .project(new Fields("documentId","term","tfidf"));
```

Because we defined the stream using `newDRPCStream`, the output of the stream will be
returned to the calling DRPC client.

There's more...

If you would like to test this quickly, update your `main` method to periodically call the DRPC
query you have just created. Take note of how the values evolve over time:

```
LocalDRPC drpc = new LocalDRPC();
    LocalCluster cluster = new LocalCluster();
    conf.setDebug(true);
    TridentTopology topology = buildTopology(null, drpc);
    cluster.submitTopology("tfidf", conf, topology.build());
    for(int i=0; i<100; i++) {
            System.out.println("DRPC RESULT: " +
                drpc.execute("tfidfQuery", "doc01 area"));
            Thread.sleep(1000);
    }
```

Integration testing of a Trident topology

In previous chapters, we have implemented integration tests by hooking into the defined
topology and providing testing bolts that allow us to exercise the topology as a black box. This
was achieved using the Java API. While this is possible with Trident, it becomes increasingly
less elegant, especially in light of the fact that there are rich testing APIs based on Clojure.

In this recipe, we will convert our pure Java project into a Polyglot project in which the Java
and Clojure code coexist comfortably. We will then implement a full integration test of the TF-
IDF topology using the Clojure testing API.

 It is assumed that the reader is familiar with Clojure and functional
programming techniques. If this is not the case, please refer to any
of the excellent online resources; however, it must be noted that
one doesn't have to be proficient at Clojure in order to implement
the integration tests. Given their simplicity and elegance, the task of
integration testing is possible with very little Clojure exposure.

How to do it...

1. Start by deleting your project from Eclipse using the Eclipse GUI and then clear the Eclipse project files:

```
mvn eclipse:clean
```

2. Once this is complete you can delete your Maven POM file. Next create a new file called `project.clj` in the root of the project:

```clojure
(defproject tfidf-topology "0.0.1-SNAPSHOT"
  :source-paths ["src/clj"]
  :java-source-paths ["src/jvm" "test/jvm"]
  :test-paths ["test/clj"]
  :javac-options    ["-target" "1.6" "-source" "1.6"]
  :resources-path "multilang"
  :aot :all
  :repositories {

              "twitter4j" "http://twitter4j.org/maven2"
              }

  :dependencies [
        [org.twitter4j/twitter4j-core "3.0.3"]
        [org.twitter4j/twitter4j-stream "3.0.3"]
        [trident-cassandra "0.0.1-wip2"]
        [org.slf4j/slf4j-log4j12 "1.6.1"]
        [com.googlecode.json-simple/json-simple "1.1"]
        [redis.clients/jedis "2.1.0"]
        [org.apache.tika/tika-parsers "1.2"]
        [org.apache.lucene/lucene-analyzers "3.6.2"]
        [org.apache.lucene/lucene-spellchecker "3.6.2"]
        [edu.washington.cs.knowitall/morpha-stemmer "1.0.4"]
        [trident-cassandra/trident-cassandra "0.0.1-wip1"]
        [commons-collections/commons-collections "3.2.1"]]

  :profiles {:dev {:dependencies [[storm "0.8.2"]
        [org.clojure/clojure "1.4.0"]
        [junit/junit "4.11"]
        [org.jmock/jmock-legacy "2.5.1"]
        [org.mockito/mockito-all "1.8.4"]
        [org.easytesting/fest-assert-core "2.0M8"]
        [net.sf.opencsv/opencsv "2.3"]
        [org.testng/testng "6.1.1"]]}}

  )
```

3. Next, you will need to refactor your folder structure to make room for the Clojure source files:

    1. Create two new folders: `src/jvm` and `src/clj`.

    2. Move the contents from `src/main/java` to `src/jvm`.

    3. Create three more folders: `test/java/`, `test/clj`, and `multilang`.

    4. Move `src/main/resource` to `multilang`.

    5. Delete `src/main`.

4. In order to enable your normal development workflow, you need to install lein and the Eclipse plugin. First download the lein script from `https://github.com/technomancy/leiningen` and add it to your path (`http://askubuntu.com/questions/60218/how-to-add-a-directory-to-my-path`).

5. Next, navigate to **Help | Install New Software | Add http://ccw.cgrand.net/updatesite/** in the Eclipse menu, complete the installation, and allow Eclipse to restart.

6. In order to import the lein project into Eclipse, you need to follow this procedure:

    1. In the project explorer go to **New | Project...**.

    2. Navigate to **General | Project**.

    3. For the project name enter `tfidf-topology`.

    4. Uncheck the **Use default location** checkbox.

    5. Browse to the location of your project and select **Finish**.

    6. Right-click on the project in the project explorer and then select **Configure | Convert to leiningen**.

Your project should now be fully available and working in Eclipse.

 If you want to change your project dependencies, simply right-click on your project in Eclipse and go to **leiningen | Reset project configuration**.

7. Next you need to add some more DRPC queries to the topology to enable our testing. Add the following methods to `TermTopology`:

```
public static void addDQueryStream(TridentState state,
TridentTopology topology, LocalDRPC drpc){
    topology.newDRPCStream("dQuery",drpc)
            .each(new Fields("args"), new Split(), new
            Fields("source"))
            .stateQuery(state, new Fields("source"), new
            MapGet(),new Fields("d"))
            .each(new Fields("d"), new FilterNull())
            .project(new Fields("source","d"));
```

```
}

    private static void addDFQueryStream(
        TridentState dfState, TridentTopology topology,
        LocalDRPC drpc) {
    topology.newDRPCStream("dfQuery",drpc)
        .each(new Fields("args"), new Split(),
            new Fields("term"))
        .stateQuery(dfState, new Fields("term"),
            new MapGet(), new Fields("df"))
        .each(new Fields("df"), new FilterNull())
        .project(new Fields("term","df"));
}
```

8. And update `buildTopology` to include these methods at the appropriate time:

```
TridentState dfState = termStream.groupBy(new Fields("term"))
        .persistentAggregate(getStateFactory("df"), new Count(),
            new Fields("df"));

    addDFQueryStream(dfState, topology, drpc);


    TridentState dState = documentStream.groupBy
        (new Fields("source"))
        .persistentAggregate(getStateFactory("d"),
        new Count(), new Fields("d"));
        addDQueryStream(dState, topology, drpc);
```

9. Finally you need to implement the integration test in Clojure. Add a file called `TermTopology.clj` to the `test/clj` folder:

```
(defn with-topology-debug* [cluster topo body-fn]
  (t/submit-local-topology (:nimbus cluster) "tester"
  {TOPOLOGY-DEBUG true} (.build topo))
  (body-fn)
  (.killTopologyWithOpts (:nimbus cluster) "tester" (doto
    (KillOptions.) (.set_wait_secs 0)))
  )

(defmacro with-topology-debug [[cluster topo] & body]
  '(with-topology-debug* ~cluster ~topo (fn [] ~@body)))

(deftest test-tfidf
    (bootstrap-db)
    (t/with-local-cluster [cluster]
      (with-drpc [drpc]
        (letlocals
```

```
(bind feeder (feeder-spout ["url"]))
(bind topo (TermTopology/buildTopology feeder drpc))
    (with-topology-debug [cluster topo]
    (feed feeder [["doc01"] ["doc02"] ["doc03"]
     ["doc04"] ["doc05"]])
    (is (= [["twitter" 5]] (exec-drpc drpc "dQuery"
        "twitter")))
    (is (= [["area" 3]] (exec-drpc drpc "dfQuery"
        "area")))
    (is (= [["doc01" "area" 0.44628710262841953]]
    (exec-drpc drpc "tfidfQuery" "doc01 area"))))))))))
```

How it works...

Leiningen is for automating Clojure projects without setting your hair on fire. It is essentially a Clojure equivalent of maven. It has many similar concepts, including dependency management. In fact, lein (short name) deploys to maven repositories and consumes dependencies from maven repositories. The important properties to take note of are:

- ▶ `source-paths`: This defines the folders containing Clojure source
- ▶ `java-source-paths`: This defines the Java source folders, both main and testing folders
- ▶ `test-paths`: This defines the Clojure testing folder
- ▶ `javac-options`: This specifies your Java compiler options
- ▶ `repositories`: This property lists external repositories to source dependencies from, over, and above the standard repos of clojars and Maven central
- ▶ `dependencies`: This property lists your dependencies; note the dependency syntax is [groupID/artefactID "version"]
- ▶ `profiles`: This allows you to specify any property only applicable to the development time

In designing the integration test, the properties that we would like to assert are the values for d, df, and `tf-idf`. We have provided DRPC queries for all of the values and therefore the integration test will treat the topology as a black box, injecting values into a spout and verifying the results using DRPC queries. Let's explore the integration test in detail to understand its functionality. Everything in Clojure is a list, typically following a form where the function name is the first entry in the list. Because functions are first-class citizens in Clojure, this is also true for defining a function (achieved by calling a function). This function is called before the tests are run in order to clear out the Cassandra database so that we can start the test with a known state.

```
(defn bootstrap-db []
  (sh "cassandra-cli" "-f" "dropAndCreateSchema.txt")
  )
```

Next, we need to declare our test, start a cluster, and initialize the DRPC server to test the topology:

```
(deftest test-tfidf
    (bootstrap-db)
    (t/with-local-cluster [cluster]
        (with-drpc [drpc]
```

with-[functionality] is a convention-based macro within the Storm testing API, which simply initializes some element and performs the functionality based on it. t/with-local-cluster, for example, is defined as follows:

```
(defmacro with-local-cluster [[cluster-sym & args] & body]
   '(let [~cluster-sym (mk-local-storm-cluster ~@args)]
      (try
        ~@body
      (catch Throwable t#
        (log-error t# "Error in cluster")
        (throw t#)
        )
      (finally
        (kill-local-storm-cluster ~cluster-sym)))
        ))
```

As you can see, the macro makes it simple to create a cluster and then execute your functionality using it; your functionality is the body passed as an argument. The naming convention simply makes tests syntactically pleasing. Next we need to create the topology and a way to inject tuples into the topology:

```
(letlocals
        (bind feeder (feeder-spout ["url"]))
        (bind topo (TermTopology/buildTopology feeder drpc))
```

feeder is a testing spout that we pass to the buildTopology method, which we can then use to inject tuples into the topology. Clojure's Java interop defines various syntactical idioms for calling Java constructs. TermTopology/buildTopology calls out the buildTopology method and passes the created spout and drpc server. Next we can feed tuples into the topology and then verify the results:

```
(with-topology-debug [cluster topo]
  (feed feeder [["doc01"] ["doc02"] ["doc03"] ["doc04"] ["doc05"]])
  (is (= [["twitter" 5]] (exec-drpc drpc "dQuery" "twitter")))
  (is (= [["area" 3]] (exec-drpc drpc "dfQuery" "area")))
  (is (= [["doc01" "area" 0.44628710262841953]] (exec-drpc drpc
    "tfidfQuery" "doc01 area")))
```

with-topology-debug is a macro that submits the topology to the local cluster, with {TOPOLOGY-DEBUG true}.

There's more...

To run the tests, you can either use the command-line REPL that can be launched using lein:

```
lein repl
```

Or you can launch the REPL in Eclipse, using the *Ctrl + Alt + S* shortcut key. Once the REPL has been launched and is in the correct namespace (this happens automatically when using Eclipse shortcut), simply call the function:

```
(run-tests)
```

 When you change any Java code you will need to restart the REPL to force it to pick them up. The command-line REPL requires that you first compile the Java source using `lein javac`.

Implementing a rolling window topology

In many temporal applications, it is important to be able answer the question of "What happened in the last X amount of time?" This is commonly referred to as a sliding window:

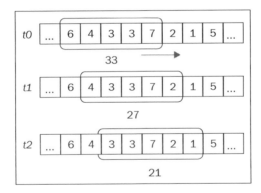

However, while working with Storm as the Speed layer of the Lambda architecture, it is required that we implement a rolling time window whereby we can segment time in a fixed manner. These fixed-time boundaries allow us to easily merge the Batch and Speed layers and provide a complete and seamless answer.

The following diagram illustrates a rolling window:

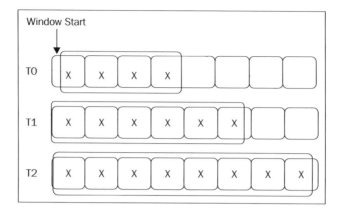

In *Chapter 6, Integrating Storm and Hadoop,* we will explore combining the results of the rolling windows with precomputed data views from the batch layer using DRPC. It must also be noted that a favorable property of the topology is that rolled windows are not immediately overwritten or discarded. This allows for a more robust implementation whereby batch processing failures can be tolerated within the speed layer.

 The time boundary would not be required if you delayed more processing until a point in time and performed the processing using DRPC only. This would mean all aggregations are created at that point in time and then discarded, which is typically not practical.

How to do it...

In *Chapter 3, Calculating Term Importance with Trident,* we used the master branch of the `trident-cassandra` project as the state implementation to persist to Cassandra.

1. In order to implement the rolling time window, we will need to use a fork of this state implementation. Start by cloning, building, and installing it into our local Maven repo:

```
git clone https://github.com/quintona/trident-cassandra.git
cd trident-cassandra
lein install
```

2. Then update your project dependencies to include this new version by changing the following code line:

```
[trident-cassandra/trident-cassandra "0.0.1-wip1"]
```

To the following line:

```
[trident-cassandra/trident-cassandra "0.0.1-bucketwip1"]
```

3. Ensure that you have updated your project dependencies in Eclipse using the process described earlier and then create a new class called TimeBasedRowStrategy:

```
public class TimeBasedRowStrategy implements RowKeyStrategy,
Serializable {
   private static final long serialVersionUID =
                                         6981400531506165681L;

   @Override
   public <T> String getRowKey(List<List<Object>> keys, Options<T>
                           options) {
      return options.rowKey + StateUtils.formatHour(new Date());
   }


}
```

4. And implement the StateUtils.formatHour static method:

```
public static String formatHour(Date date){
    return new SimpleDateFormat("yyyyMMddHH").format(date);
   }
```

5. Finally, replace the getStateFactory method in TermTopology with the following:

```
private static StateFactory getStateFactory(String rowKey) {
    CassandraBucketState.BucketOptions options = new
CassandraBucketState.BucketOptions();
    options.keyspace = "trident_test";
    options.columnFamily = "tfid";
    options.rowKey = rowKey;
    options.keyStrategy = new TimeBasedRowStrategy();
    return CassandraBucketState.nonTransactional("localhost",
          options);
   }
```

How it works...

The standard implementation of the map state through the `trident-cassandra` state implementation assumes a set `rowKey` per row in your column family. There is therefore a relationship between the map state at the Trident level and a single row within the column family at a Cassandra level. The fork of the state implementation adds a bucket capability. Essentially this means that you can dynamically specify the row key that will be used for the state at runtime, using a row key strategy that you provide. Logically this gives us the ability to partition our state without introducing an extra layer of complexity in our topology logic. The strategy implementation in this case will logically partition our state based on hours, by returning a concatenated combination of both the static row key and a representation of the current hour.

```
public <T> String getRowKey(List<List<Object>> keys, Options<T>
options) {
    return options.rowKey + StateUtils.formatHour(new Date());
}
```

Therefore, at the Trident level, all state updates are partitioned by this hour. So, as the value for d is incremented, it is only incremented for this hour; the same is true of the values for `df`.

Note that any time partition could have been selected. It can easily be changed to using daily slots by introducing a `formatDay` method based on the current time.

 This functionality enables the goal of keeping the values for previous time windows; however, this also implies that separate a housekeeping functionality must be put in place to clean out windows that are no longer required because they have been taken into account in the Batch layer.

Simulating time in integration testing

A vital property of any automated test is that it is consistent and repeatable. In other words, it must either fail or succeed consistently. This can make testing temporal applications difficult because of the fact that time is always different between test runs. In order to create stable tests, it is important to simulate the time within the cluster so that the integration tests can advance the time by specific amounts and explicitly test all the boundary conditions. The trident testing API fully enables such a test scenario; this recipe will explore the minor changes required to be made to the topology under test and the actual integration tests.

How to do it...

1. First you need to enable your topology for simulated time. Change the `getRowKey` string in the `TimeBasedRowStrategy` method to the following:

```
public <T> String getRowKey(List<List<Object>> keys, Options<T>
options) {
    return options.rowKey + StateUtils.formatHour(new Date(Time
        .currentTimeMillis()));
}
```

2. And then update the integration test as follows:

```
(deftest test-tfidf
    (bootstrap-db)
    (t/with-simulated-time-local-cluster [cluster]
        (with-drpc [drpc]
            (letlocals
                (bind feeder (feeder-spout ["url"]))
                (bind topo (TermTopology/buildTopology feeder
                  drpc))
                (with-topology-debug [cluster topo]
                    (feed feeder [["doc01"] ["doc02"] ["doc03"]
                        ["doc04"] ["doc05"]])
                    (is (= [["twitter" 5]] (exec-drpc drpc
                        "dQuery" "twitter")))
                    (is (= [["area" 3]] (exec-drpc drpc "dfQuery"
                        "area")))
                    (is (= [["doc01" "area" 0.44628710262841953]]
                        (exec-drpc drpc "tfidfQuery" "doc01 area")))
                    (t/advance-time-secs! 5400)
                    (feed feeder [["doc01"] ["doc02"] ["doc03"]
                        ["doc04"] ["doc05"]])
                    (is (= [["twitter" 5]] (exec-drpc drpc
                        "dQuery" "twitter")))
                    (is (= [["area" 3]] (exec-drpc drpc "dfQuery"
                        "area")))
                    (is (= [["doc01" "area" 0.44628710262841953]]
                (exec-drpc drpc "tfidfQuery" "doc01 area")))))))))
```

How it works...

Storm ships with some utility classes to enable the simulated time within the cluster. To take advantage of this, you simply have to use `Time.currentTimeMillis()` from `backtype.storm.utils.Time`, instead of using the system time method calls. Within your integration test, we are using the local cluster with the simulated time instead of the actual time. The nature of the test is also different now. In order to test the time bucket, we will perform the following steps:

1. Start at time `0` and inject a series of tuples.

2. Verify the resulting values for `d`, `df`, and `tf-idf`.

3. Move the time forward by more than an hour.

4. Inject another set of tuples.

5. Verify that the resulting values for `d`, `df`, and `tf-idf` are not related in any way.

To expand on this, if the bucket functionality wasn't in place and this test was run, the resulting value for `d` would be `5` at the first DRPC execution and then `10` at the second DRPC execution. However, with the bucket functionality in place, the value for `d` should be `5` in both cases due to the state being entirely partitioned at the Cassandra level.

5
Polyglot Topology

In this chapter, we will cover:

- ▶ Implementing the multilang protocol in Qt
- ▶ Implementing the SplitSentence bolt in Qt
- ▶ Implementing the count bolt in Ruby
- ▶ Defining the word count topology in Clojure

Introduction

We break away briefly from the TF-IDF thread to explore the polyglot capabilities of Storm. Polyglot development is becoming increasingly important, particularly in the open source world where mashups present a rapid path to delivery, regardless of the underlying technology. There is an increasing number of JVM-based languages that maintain binary-level compatibility with Java, such as Scala. In these cases, the Polyglot project is simply a composition of JAR files with appropriate levels of modularity. In the cases where the underlying execution environment isn't common, other approaches are required. There are many use cases, over and above convenient re-use, such as high-performance computing, where native implementations provide for greater levels of optimization or leverage of low-level hardware capabilities, such as the rich functionality of GPUs, in most modern PCs.

There are many approaches to integrating systems developed in incompatible languages, including messaging, sockets, and Apache Thrift. As a real-time system, Storm is shipped with a very lean multi-language protocol, with implementations for Ruby and Python. This protocol is described fully on the Storm wiki at `https://github.com/nathanmarz/storm/wiki/Multilang-protocol`. This chapter presents a Polyglot topology that, while not being very useful, does fully present the power of Storm in delivering a multi-language-based system, including the construction of a multilang adaptor. The example used is the canonical word count topology where the topology will be defined in Clojure and the bolts will be implemented in C++ and Ruby.

Implementing the multilang protocol in Qt

The multilang protocol is extremely trivial in nature. It consists of JSON-based exchanges over STDIN and STDOUT. All exchanges are delimited via a single line containing the word end, which isn't JSON-encoded. In this recipe, we will only implement the bolt adaptor; however, adding the spout functionality is trivial from this base.

The bolt can receive new tuple messages that contain an ID, some component metadata, and the actual tuple as a JSON value containing a JSON array of values. The bolt then sends ack, fail, emit, or log messages back via STDOUT.

Qt is an open source C++ framework, originally developed by Trolltech as a cross-platform GUI framework. Qt has enjoyed impressive longevity in the open source communities, providing a wide range of cross-platform C++ capability. This functionality extends far beyond GUI concerns into base container classes and Threads; it even augments the C++ language with some missing elements, such as reflection and reference counting-based memory management. It is, therefore, a convenient framework to partner with Java where required as it supports all the operating systems that Java does.

 It must be noted that C++ doesn't automatically equate to better-performing code. The JVM's JIT compiler does an impressive job and as a result Java code will outperform the C++ code that is written in an "average" manner in many cases. The XML DOM parsers were a good example of this for many years where the C++-implemented code had simply been ported from Java.

Getting ready

In order to get ready for this recipe, we simply need to install the Qt SDK; you can easily do this using apt-get.

```
sudo apt-get install qt-sdk
```

How to do it...

We are going to implement the logic to comply with the Storm multilang protocol using Qt. In order to do this, we will start by creating a new Qt project.

1. Create a folder for the C++ project and create a Qt Project file.

   ```
   mkdir splitsentence-cpp-bolt
   cd splitsentence-cpp-bolt
   vim splitsentence-cpp-bolt.pro
   ```

2. The .pro file is the Qt makefile or the project file. Add the following content to it:

```
TEMPLATE = app
TARGET = splitsentence-cpp-bolt
# Input
HEADERS += \
    qtuple.h \
    qbasicbolt.h
SOURCES += main.cpp \
    qbasicbolt.cpp
```

3. You must then create a tuple header file named qtuple.h.

```
class QTuple
{

private:
    QString id;
    QString component;
    QString stream;
    int task;
    QJsonValue* value;
};
```

 Note that the code does not use C++ 11 features, such as delegate constructors; this would be an obvious improvement if you have already chosen to upgrade.

4. Next, you must define the QBasicBolt class starting with the header file definition.

```
class QBasicBolt : public QObject
{
 virtual void process(QTuple *tuple) = 0;

    void start();

private:
    QQueue<QJsonValue*> pending_taskids;
    QQueue<QJsonValue*> pending_commands;

protected:
    virtual QString readLine();
    virtual void sendMsgToParent(QJsonValue &v);
    QTuple* readTuple();
    QJsonValue *emitTuple(QTuple *tuple);
};
```

Please note that the `readLine` and `sendMsgToParent` methods have both been marked as `virtual`. This was done to make this class more testable where a unit test could mock out these functions and perform an in-process black box test of the class. These methods represent the input and output points of the class.

5. Next, you must provide the class implementation.

```cpp
void QBasicBolt::start()
{
    QPair<QJsonValue*, QJsonValue*> conf_context =
InitComponent();
    initialize(conf_context.first, conf_context.second);
    run();
}

void QBasicBolt::run()
{
    while(true){
        QTuple* tuple = readTuple();
        if(tuple != NULL)
        {
            anchor_tuple = tuple;
            ack(tuple->getId());
            process(tuple);
            delete tuple;
        } else
        {
            QThread::sleep(50);
        }
    }
}

void QBasicBolt::sendMsgToParent(QJsonValue &v)
{
    QJsonDocument *doc;
    if(v.isArray()){
        doc = new QJsonDocument(v.toArray());
    } else {
        doc = new QJsonDocument(v.toObject());
    }
    std::cout << doc->toJson().constData();
    std::cout << "end" << std::endl;
    delete doc;
}
```

```cpp
QString QBasicBolt::readLine()
{
    bool readLine = false;
    std::string temp;
    getline(std::cin, temp).good();
    QString line = QString::fromStdString(temp);
    if (readLine && (line != "end"))
        line = line + "\n";
    return line;
}


QTuple* QBasicBolt::readTuple()
{
    QJsonValue* msg = readCommand();
    if(msg == NULL)
        return NULL;
    if(msg->isObject()){
        QJsonObject obj = msg->toObject();
        return new QTuple(obj["id"].toString(), obj["comp"]
                        .toString(), obj["stream"].toString(),
                        (int)obj["task"].toDouble(),obj
                        .value("tuple"));
    }
    return NULL;
}


void QBasicBolt::emitBolt(QTuple *tuple,
                        const QString &stream, int task)
{
    QJsonObject obj;
    obj.insert(QString("command"),QString("emit"));
    if (!stream.isEmpty())
        obj.insert(QString("stream"),stream);
    if (task != -1)
        obj.insert(QString("task"),task);
    obj.insert(QString("tuple"), *tuple->getValue());
    QJsonValue v(obj);
    sendMsgToParent(v);
}
```

How it works...

This class provides the implementation of the multilang protocol. It abstracts this complexity away from the implementing subclass, thereby allowing it to simply implement the executable method with the appropriate bolt logic. A compiled executable will be invoked by the ShellBolt class that ships with Storm. The ShellBolt class will act as a parent for the duration of the execution, exchanging commands and tuples with the concrete instance of the QBasicBolt class. The ShellBolt class essentially delegates the logic to this externally provided bolt. The details of ShellBolt are presented in the next recipe; for the moment, it is sufficient to understand that a Java class will start the process and exchange messages via STDIN and STDOUT with the concrete instance of QBasicBolt.

The bolt starts by initializing and placing a PID file, which will be used for process management.

```
void QBasicBolt::start()
{
    QPair<QJsonValue*, QJsonValue*> conf_context = InitComponent();
    initialize(conf_context.first, conf_context.second);
    run();
}
```

It then enters into a permanent loop of consuming tuples and generating responses.

```
void QBasicBolt::run()
{
    while(true){
        QTuple* tuple = readTuple();
        if(tuple != NULL)
        {
            anchor_tuple = tuple;
            ack(tuple->getId());
            process(tuple);
            delete tuple;
        } else
        {
            QThread::sleep(50);
        }
    }
}
```

The tuples received are first acknowledged and then processed. Note that the process method is defined as a pure virtual function and must be provided by the concrete instance. The class also provides convenience methods to be able to emit tuples, logs, and failures.

Care must be taken to generate the appropriate JSON elements of the tuple by the concrete instance in accordance with the specification on wiki; however, if inappropriate messages are generated, the topology will fail rapidly as it should.

Implementing the SplitSentence bolt in Qt

The **SplitSentence** bolt is embarrassingly simple, which is important for canonical examples. Remember that the point is to focus on the creation of the multilang adaptor. The bolt simply reads the sentence from the tuple, tokenizes the sentence based on spaces, and emits each word.

How to do it...

1. Create the concrete implementation of `QBasicBolt` named `SplitSentence` starting with the header.

```cpp
#ifndef SPLITSENTENCE_H
#define SPLITSENTENCE_H

#include <QObject>
#include "qbasicbolt.h"

class SplitSentence : public QBasicBolt
{
    Q_OBJECT
public:
    explicit SplitSentence(QObject *parent = 0);

    void initialize(QJsonValue* conf, QJsonValue* context) { }
    void process(QTuple *tuple);

signals:

public slots:

};

#endif // SPLITSENTENCE_H
```

2. Next, provide the implementation of the `process` method:

```cpp
void SplitSentence::process(QTuple *tuple)
{
    QJsonArray val = tuple->getValue()->toArray();
    QString s = val.at(0).toString();
    QStringList tokens = s.split(" ");
    for (QStringList::Iterator i = tokens.begin(); i != tokens
        .end(); ++i)
    {
        QJsonValue value(*i);
        QTuple* t = new QTuple(value);
        QJsonValue* result = emitTuple(t);
        if(result != NULL)
            delete result;
        delete t;
    }
}
```

3. Afterwards, you need to make the bolt executable. This is done by completing the implementation of the `main` method in the `main.cpp` file.

```cpp
int main(int argc, char *argv[])
{
    QCoreApplication app(argc, argv);
    SplitSentence b;
    b.start();
    return 0;
}
```

4. Then, update the `.pro` file to reflect the following changes:

```
TEMPLATE = app
TARGET = splitsentence-cpp-bolt
# Input
HEADERS += \
    qtuple.h \
    qbasicbolt.h \
    splitsentence.h
SOURCES += main.cpp \
    qbasicbolt.cpp \
    splitsentence.cpp
```

5. Finally, the build process involves generating a platform-specific makefile and then building the executable. Perform the following commands within the `project` folder:

qmake

make

How it works...

The bolt simply extracts the sentence from the tuple, splits it, and then emits those words as separate tuples. There are a few things to note for those who are familiar with the Java API.

Firstly, the values are passed into the `process` method as a JSON value within the method. Secondly, at this level, we don't have any idea of the field names of the fields; therefore, you need to access each value in the input tuple based on the value index within the array. Finally, the value that you emit must also be a JSON array, otherwise the bolt's parent will fail to process the command.

For those with a Java background, the code will be legible. A few points to consider while making changes and experimenting are as follows:

- C++ separates out the definition of the class from its implementation. This allows the implementation to be included in many places and is still correctly addressed with the help of the details in the header. You can provide implementations inside the header file; however, you must remember that the implementation will be included in every library that it is included in, resulting in potential conflicts and bloated footprints.

- The macro definitions at the start and end of the header files are vital to prevent the compiler from seeing the header as a duplicate definition each time it is included.

- Memory must be managed. Prefer values on the stack, pass by reference, and, when allocating onto the stack, ensure that you have a delete instruction to free the memory or that it is appropriately parented.

There's more...

In order to expose the Qt-based bolt to the topology, we need to provide the Java-based parent bolt. To achieve this, you further need to create a project called `polyglot-count-topology`. Within the `src/jvm/storm/cookbook`, create the following class:

```
package storm.cookbook;

import java.util.Map;

import backtype.storm.task.ShellBolt;
import backtype.storm.topology.IRichBolt;
import backtype.storm.topology.OutputFieldsDeclarer;
import backtype.storm.tuple.Fields;

public class QtSplitSentence extends ShellBolt implements IRichBolt {

    private static final long serialVersionUID = -2503812433333011106L;
```

```
        public QtSplitSentence() {
            super("splitsentence-cpp-bolt");
        }


        @Override
        public void declareOutputFields(OutputFieldsDeclarer declarer) {
            declarer.declare(new Fields("word"));
        }


        @Override
        public Map<String, Object> getComponentConfiguration() {
            return null;
        }


    }
```

The parent simply declares the fields and defines the command to be run. The final step is to create a folder named `resources` within the `polyglot-count-topology` project under `multilang` and place the compiled executable file in it.

> In a production situation, you would need to ensure the Storm nodes are appropriately provisioned with Qt binaries; otherwise, the compiled executable will fail to run when the topology is deployed onto the cluster. The provisioning scripts provided in *Chapter 1, Setting Up your Development Environment*, would be a good starting point for this.

Implementing the count bolt in Ruby

The Ruby bolt is also very simple given that Storm ships with an implementation of the multilang adaptor for Ruby.

How to do it...

1. In the `resources` folder under `multilang`, create a Ruby file called `count.rb` with the following content:

    ```ruby
    require "./storm"

    class CountBolt < Storm::Bolt
      attr_accessor :counts
      def initialize
        @counts = Hash.new
      end
    ```

```ruby
  def process(tup)
    word = String(tup.values[0])
    counts[:word] = counts[:word].to_i + 1.to_i
    emit([word, counts[:word].to_s])
  end
end
```

```ruby
CountBolt.new.run
```

2. Copy the Storm multilang adaptor in the same folder. The adaptor can be copied from the Storm start project (`http://github.com/nathanmarz/storm-starter.git`). It can be found under `multilang/resources/`. Finally, you need to create the Java parent for this bolt under `src/jvm/storm/cookbook`.

```java
package storm.cookbook;

import java.util.Map;

import backtype.storm.task.ShellBolt;
import backtype.storm.topology.IRichBolt;
import backtype.storm.topology.OutputFieldsDeclarer;
import backtype.storm.tuple.Fields;

public class RubyCount extends ShellBolt implements IRichBolt {

    private static final long serialVersionUID =
                                        -5880076377355349028L;

    public RubyCount() {
        super("ruby","count.rb");
    }

    @Override
    public void declareOutputFields(OutputFieldsDeclarer declarer)
    {
        declarer.declare(new Fields("word", "count"));
    }

    @Override
    public Map<String, Object> getComponentConfiguration() {
        return null;
    }

}
```

How it works...

The Ruby bolt extends the Storm bolt and implements the `process` method. A member-level hash map holds the counts for each word. This map is incremented and the new total is emitted as each word is received.

Take note of the number of parameters passed to the parent constructor in the parent bolt.

 As with the Qt example, you must ensure that the appropriate version of Ruby is provisioned on your nodes or this will fail.

Defining the word count topology in Clojure

To close off, we need to define the topology using Clojure. Remember that the point of this topology is to drive home the polyglot nature of Storm. You can deliver multi-technology real-time topologies and you must select the appropriate method. The bolts described earlier in this chapter used the minimal multilang protocol. There are various other ways, including Thrift, the Clojure's Java interop, and, in the case of Qt, you could have easily used the Qt Jambi project. The selection of the appropriate method depends on many factors within your environment. Use the right tool for the right job.

How to do it...

1. Create the Lein project file within the `polyglot-count-topology` project folder, and name the file `project.clj`.

```
(defproject polyglot-count-topology "0.0.1-SNAPSHOT"
  :source-paths ["src/clj"]
  :java-source-paths ["src/jvm" "test/jvm"]
  :test-paths ["test/clj"]
  :javac-options     ["-target" "1.6" "-source" "1.6"]
  :resource-paths ["multilang"]
  :main storm.cookbook.count-topology
  :aot :all
  :min-lein-version "2.0.0"
  :dependencies [[org.slf4j/slf4j-log4j12 "1.6.1"]
                 [org.clojure/clojure "1.4.0"]
                 [commons-collections/commons-collections "3.2.1"]
                 [storm-starter "0.0.1-SNAPSHOT"]]
```

```
:profiles {:dev {:dependencies [[storm "0.8.2"]
                    [junit/junit "4.11"]
                    [org.testng/testng "6.1.1"]]}}


)
```

2. Within the `src/clj/storm/cookbook` folder, create the Clojure topology named `count_topology.clj`.

```
(ns storm.cookbook.count-topology
  (:import (backtype.storm StormSubmitter LocalCluster)
           (storm.cookbook QtSplitSentence RubyCount))
  (:use [backtype.storm clojure config])
  )

(defspout sentence-spout ["sentence"]
  [conf context collector]
  (let [sentences ["a little brown dog"
                   "the man petted the dog"
                   "four score and seven years ago"
                   "an apple a day keeps the doctor away"]]
    (spout
     (nextTuple []
       (Thread/sleep 100)
       (emit-spout! collector [(rand-nth sentences)])
       )
     (ack [id]
       )))))

(defn mk-topology []

  (topology
   {"1" (spout-spec sentence-spout)}
   {"3" (bolt-spec {"1" :shuffle}
                   (QtSplitSentence.)
                   :p 1)
    "4" (bolt-spec {"3" ["word"]}
                   (RubyCount.)
                   :p 1)}))

(defn run-local! []
  (let [cluster (LocalCluster.)]
    (.submitTopology cluster "word-count" {TOPOLOGY-DEBUG true}
(mk-topology))
```

```
          (Thread/sleep 10000)
          (.shutdown cluster)
          ))

    (defn submit-topology! [name]
      (StormSubmitter/submitTopology
        name
        {TOPOLOGY-DEBUG true
         TOPOLOGY-WORKERS 3}
        (mk-topology)))

    (defn -main
      ([]
       (run-local!))
      ([name]
       (submit-topology! name)))
```

How it works...

We define a spout for testing purposes that emits the sentences:

```
(defspout sentence-spout ["sentence"]
  [conf context collector]
  (let [sentences ["a little brown dog"
                   "the man petted the dog"
                   "four score and seven years ago"
                   "an apple a day keeps the doctor away"]]
    (spout
     (nextTuple []
       (Thread/sleep 100)
       (emit-spout! collector [(rand-nth sentences)])
       )
     (ack [id]
       ))))
```

We then define the topology:

```
(topology
   {"1" (spout-spec sentence-spout)}
   {"3" (bolt-spec {"1" :shuffle}
                   (QtSplitSentence.)
                   :p 1)
    "4" (bolt-spec {"3" ["word"]}
                   (RubyCount.)
                   :p 1)}))
```

The body of the function adds elements to the topology, starting with the spout, and then adds the two bolts, which we have defined earlier in the chapter. Note that we simply create instances of the bolts that are the Java parents of the underlying bolt implementation, using the Clojure's Java interop notation for creating a new instance of the class RubyCount.

There's more...

You can now execute the topology. At the command line, execute the following commands:

```
lein deps
lein javac
lein compile
lein repl
```

Once the REPL has launched, execute the run-local! function and the topology will launch and execute. You can use this command to package the deployable JAR file for you.

```
lein uberjar
```

6

Integrating Storm
and Hadoop

In this chapter, we will cover:

- ▸ Implementing TF-IDF in Hadoop
- ▸ Persisting documents from Storm
- ▸ Integrating the batch and real-time views

Introduction

In *Chapter 4, Distributed Remote Procedure Calls*, we implemented the Speed layer for a Lambda architecture instance using Storm. In this chapter, we will implement the Batch and Service layers to complete the architecture.

There are some key concepts underlying this big data architecture:

- ▸ Immutable state
- ▸ Abstraction and composition
- ▸ Constrain complexity

Immutable state is the key, in that it provides true fault-tolerance for the architecture. If a failure is experienced at any level, we can always rebuild the data from the original immutable data. This is in contrast to many existing data systems, where the paradigm is to act on mutable data. This approach may seem simple and logical; however, it exposes the system to a particular kind of risk in which the state is lost or corrupted. It also constrains the system, in that you can only work with the current view of the data; it isn't possible to derive new views of the data. When the architecture is based on a fundamentally immutable state, it becomes both flexible and fault-tolerant.

Abstractions allow us to remove complexity in some cases, and in others they can introduce complexity. It is important to achieve an appropriate set of abstractions that increase our productivity and remove complexity, but at an appropriate cost. It must be noted that all abstractions *leak*, meaning that when failures occur at a lower abstraction, they will affect the higher-level abstractions. It is therefore often important to be able to make changes within the various layers and understand more than one layer of abstraction. The designs we choose to implement our abstractions must therefore not prevent us from reasoning about or working at the lower levels of abstraction when required. Open source projects are often good at this, because of the obvious access to the code of the lower level abstractions, but even with source code available, it is easy to convolute the abstraction to the extent that it becomes a risk. In a big data solution, we have to work at higher levels of abstraction in order to be productive and deal with the massive complexity, so we need to choose our abstractions carefully. In the case of Storm, Trident represents an appropriate abstraction for dealing with the data-processing complexity, but the lower level Storm API on which Trident is based isn't hidden from us. We are therefore able to easily reason about Trident based on an understanding of lower-level abstractions within Storm.

Another key issue to consider when dealing with complexity and productivity is composition. **Composition** within a given layer of abstraction allows us to quickly build out a solution that is well tested and easy to reason about. Composition is fundamentally decoupled, while abstraction contains some inherent coupling to the lower-level abstractions—something that we need to be aware of.

Finally, a big data solution needs to constrain complexity. Complexity always equates to risk and cost in the long run, both from a development perspective and from an operational perspective. Real-time solutions will always be more complex than batch-based systems; they also lack some of the qualities we require in terms of performance. Nathan Marz's Lambda architecture attempts to address this by combining the qualities of each type of system to constrain complexity and deliver a truly fault-tolerant architecture.

In *Chapter 3, Calculating Term Importance with Trident*, and *Chapter 4, Distributed Remote Procedure Calls*, we implemented a real-time TF-IDF data flow using Trident. We divided this flow into preprocessing and "at time" phases, using streams and DRPC streams respectively. We also introduced time windows that allowed us to segment the preprocessed data. In this chapter, we complete the entire architecture by implementing the Batch and Service layers.

The Service layer is simply a store of a view of the data. In this case, we will store this view in Cassandra, as it is a convenient place to access the state alongside Trident's state. The preprocessed view is identical to the preprocessed view created by Trident, counted elements of the TF-IDF formula (D, DF, and TF), but in the batch case, the dataset is much larger, as it includes the entire history.

The Batch layer is implemented in Hadoop using MapReduce to calculate the preprocessed view of the data. MapReduce is extremely powerful, but like the lower-level Storm API, is potentially too low-level for the problem at hand for the following reasons:

- ▸ We need to describe the problem as a data pipeline; MapReduce isn't congruent with such a way of thinking
- ▸ Productivity

We would like to think of a data pipeline in terms of streams of data, tuples within the stream and predicates acting on those tuples. This allows us to easily describe a solution to a data processing problem, but it also promotes composability, in that predicates are fundamentally composable, but pipelines themselves can also be composed to form larger, more complex pipelines. Cascading provides such an abstraction for MapReduce in the same way as Trident does for Storm.

With these tools, approaches, and considerations in place, we can now complete our real-time big data architecture. There are a number of elements from *Chapter 3*, *Calculating Term Importance with Trident*, and *Chapter 4*, *Distributed Remote Procedure Calls*, that we will update, and a number of elements that we will add. The following figure illustrates the final architecture, where the elements in light grey will be updated from the existing recipe, and the elements in dark grey will be added in this chapter:

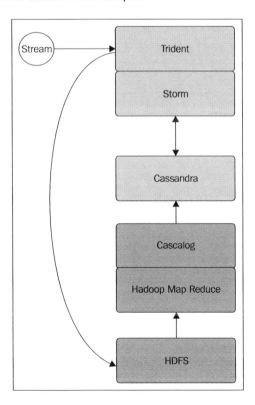

Implementing TF-IDF in Hadoop

TF-IDF is a well-known problem in the MapReduce communities; it is well-documented and implemented, and it is interesting in that it is sufficiently complex to be useful and instructive at the same time. Cascading has a series of tutorials on TF-IDF at `http://www.cascading. org/2012/07/31/cascading-for-the-impatient-part-5/`, which documents this implementation well. For this recipe, we shall use a Clojure **Domain Specific Language** (**DSL**) called Cascalog that is implemented on top of Cascading. Cascalog has been chosen because it provides a set of abstractions that are very semantically similar to the Trident API and are very terse while still remaining very readable and easy to understand.

Getting ready

Before you begin, please ensure that you have installed Hadoop by following the instructions at `http://www.michael-noll.com/tutorials/running-hadoop-on-ubuntu-linux-single-node-cluster/`.

How to do it...

1. Start by creating the project using the `lein` command:

   ```
   lein new tfidf-cascalog
   ```

2. Next, you need to edit the `project.clj` file to include the dependencies:

   ```
   (defproject tfidf-cascalog "0.1.0-SNAPSHOT"
   :dependencies [[org.clojure/clojure "1.4.0"]
                  [cascalog "1.10.1"]
                  [org.apache.cassandra/cassandra-all "1.1.5"]
                  [clojurewerkz/cassaforte "1.0.0-beta11-SNAPSHOT"]
                  [quintona/cascading-cassandra "0.0.7-SNAPSHOT"]
                  [clj-time "0.5.0"]
                  [cascading.avro/avro-scheme "2.2-SNAPSHOT"]
                  [cascalog-more-taps "0.3.0"]
                  [org.apache.httpcomponents/httpclient "4.2.3"]]
   :profiles { :dev {:dependencies [[org.apache.hadoop/hadoop-core
                                     "0.20.2-dev"]
                                    [lein-midje "3.0.1"]
                                    [cascalog/midje-cascalog
                                    "1.10.1"]]}})
   ```

   It is always a good idea to validate your dependencies; to do this, execute `lein deps` and review any errors. In this particular case, `cascading-cassandra` has not been deployed to clojars, and so you will receive an error message. Simply download the source from `https://github.com/quintona/cascading-cassandra` and install it into your local repository using Maven.

3. It is also good practice to understand your dependency tree. This is important to not only prevent duplicate classpath issues, but also to understand what licenses you are subject to. To do this, simply run `lein pom`, followed by `mvn dependency:tree`. You can then review the tree for conflicts. In this particular case, you will notice that there are two conflicting versions of Avro. You can fix this by adding the appropriate exclusions:

```
[org.apache.cassandra/cassandra-all "1.1.5"
        :exclusions [org.apache.cassandra.deps/avro]]
```

4. We then need to create the Clojure-based Cascade queries that will process the document data. We first need to create the query that will create the "D" view of the data; that is, the D portion of the TF-IDF function. This is achieved by defining a Cascalog function that will output a key and a value, which is composed of a set of predicates:

```
(defn D [src]
    (let [src   (select-fields src ["?doc-id"])]
      (<- [?key ?d-str]
          (src ?doc-id)
          (c/distinct-count ?doc-id :> ?n-docs)
          (str "twitter" :> ?key)
          (str ?n-docs :> ?d-str))))
```

You can define this and any of the following functions in the REPL, or add them to `core.clj` in your project. If you want to use the REPL, simply use `lein repl` from within the `project` folder. The required namespace (the `use` statement), `require`, and `import` definitions can be found in the source code bundle.

5. We then need to add similar functions to calculate the TF and DF values:

```
(defn DF [src]
    (<- [?key ?df-count-str]
        (src ?doc-id ?time ?df-word)
        (c/distinct-count ?doc-id ?df-word :> ?df-count)
        (str ?df-word :> ?key)
        (str ?df-count :> ?df-count-str)))

(defn TF [src]
    (<- [?key ?tf-count-str]
        (src ?doc-id ?time ?tf-word)
        (c/count ?tf-count)
        (str ?doc-id ?tf-word :> ?key)
        (str ?tf-count :> ?tf-count-str)))
```

6. This Batch layer is only interested in calculating views for all the data leading up to, but not including, the current hour. This is because the data for the current hour will be provided by Trident when it merges this batch view with the view it has calculated. In order to achieve this, we need to filter out all the records that are within the current hour. The following function makes that possible:

```
(deffilterop timing-correct? [doc-time]
  (let [now (local-now)
        interval (in-minutes (interval (from-long doc-time) now))]
    (if (< interval 60) false true))
```

7. Each of the preceding query definitions require a clean stream of words. The text contained in the source documents isn't clean. It still contains stop words. In order to filter these and emit a clean set of words for these queries, we can compose a function that splits the text into words and filters them based on a list of stop words and the time function defined previously:

```
(defn etl-docs-gen [rain stop]
  (<- [?doc-id ?time ?word]
      (rain ?doc-id ?time ?line)
      (split ?line :> ?word-dirty)
      ((c/comp s/trim s/lower-case) ?word-dirty :> ?word)
      (stop ?word :> false)
      (timing-correct? ?time)))
```

8. We will be storing the outputs from our queries to Cassandra, which requires us to define a set of taps for these views:

```
(defn create-tap [rowkey cassandra-ip]
  (let [keyspace storm_keyspace
        column-family "tfidfbatch"
        scheme          (CassandraScheme. cassandra-ip
                                           "9160"
                                           keyspace
                                           column-family
                                           rowkey
                                           {
"cassandra.inputPartitioner" "org.apache.cassandra.dht.
RandomPartitioner" "cassandra.outputPartitioner" "org.apache.
cassandra.dht.RandomPartitioner"})
        tap             (CassandraTap. scheme)]
    tap))

(defn create-d-tap [cassandra-ip]
  (create-tap "d"cassandra-ip))

(defn create-df-tap [cassandra-ip]
```

```
(create-tap "df" cassandra-ip))

(defn create-tf-tap [cassandra-ip]
  (create-tap "tf" cassandra-ip))
```

 The way this schema is created means that it will use a static row key and persist name-value pairs from the tuples as `column:value` within that row. This is congruent with the approach used by the Trident Cassandra adaptor. This is a convenient approach, as it will make our lives easier later.

9. We can complete the implementation by a providing a function that ties everything together and executes the queries:

```
(defn execute [in stop cassandra-ip]
  (cc/connect! cassandra-ip)
  (sch/set-keyspace storm_keyspace)
  (let [input (tap/hfs-tap (AvroScheme. (load-schema)) in)
        stop (hfs-delimited stop :skip-header? true)
        src  (etl-docs-gen input stop)]
    (?- (create-d-tap cassandra-ip)
        (D src))
    (?- (create-df-tap cassandra-ip)
        (DF src))
    (?- (create-tf-tap cassandra-ip)
        (TF src))))
```

10. Next, we need to get some data to test with. I have created some test data, which is available at `https://bitbucket.org/qanderson/tfidf-cascalog`. Simply download the project and copy the contents of `src/data` to the `data` folder in your project structure.

11. We can now test this entire implementation. To do this, we need to insert the data into Hadoop:

    `hadoop fs -copyFromLocal ./data/document.avro data/document.avro`

    `hadoop fs -copyFromLocal ./data/en.stop data/en.stop`

12. Then launch the execution from the REPL:

    `=> (execute "data/document"  "data/en.stop" "127.0.0.1")`

How it works...

There are many excellent guides on the Cascalog wiki (`https://github.com/nathanmarz/cascalog/wiki`), but for completeness's sake, the nature of a Cascalog query will be explained here. Before that, however, a revision of Cascading pipelines is required.

The following is quoted from the Cascading documentation (`http://docs.cascading.org/cascading/2.1/userguide/htmlsingle/`):

> *Pipe assemblies define what work should be done against tuple streams, which are read from tap sources and written to tap sinks. The work performed on the data stream may include actions such as filtering, transforming, organizing, and calculating. Pipe assemblies may use multiple sources and multiple sinks, and may define splits, merges, and joins to manipulate the tuple streams.*

This concept is embodied in Cascalog through the definition of queries. A **query** takes a set of inputs and applies a list of predicates across the fields in each tuple of the input stream. Queries are composed through the application of many predicates. Queries can also be composed to form larger, more complex queries. In either event, these queries are reduced down into a Cascading pipeline. Cascalog therefore provides an extremely terse and powerful abstraction on top of Cascading; moreover, it enables an excellent development workflow through the REPL. Queries can be easily composed and executed against smaller representative datasets within the REPL, providing the idiomatic API and development workflow that makes Clojure beautiful.

If we unpack the query we defined for TF, we will find the following code:

```
(defn DF [src]
  (<- [?key ?df-count-str]
      (src ?doc-id ?time ?df-word)
      (c/distinct-count ?doc-id ?df-word :> ?df-count)
      (str ?df-word :> ?key)
      (str ?df-count :> ?df-count-str)))
```

The `<-` macro defines a query, but does not execute it. The initial vector, `[?key ?df-count-str]`, defines the output fields, which is followed by a list of predicate functions. Each predicate can be one of the following three types:

- **Generators**: A source of data where the underlying source is either a tap or another query.

- **Operations**: Implicit relations that take in input variables defined elsewhere and either act as a function that binds new variables or a filter. Operations typically act within the scope of a single tuple.

- **Aggregators**: Functions that act across tuples to create aggregate representations of data. For example, `count` and `sum`.

The `:>` keyword is used to separate input variables from output variables. If no `:>` keyword is specified, the variables are considered as input variables for operations and output variables for generators and aggregators.

The `(src ?doc-id ?time ?df-word)` predicate function names the first three values within the input tuple, whose names are applicable within the query scope. Therefore, if the tuple (`"doc1"` `123324` `"This"`) arrives in this query, the variables would effectively bind as follows:

- ► `?doc-id:` `"doc1"`
- ► `?time:` `123324`
- ► `?df-word:` `"This"`

Each predicate within the scope of the query can use any bound value or add new bound variables to the scope of the query. The final set of bound values that are emitted is defined by the output vector.

We defined three queries, each calculating a portion of the value required for the TF-IDF algorithm. These are fed from two single taps, which are files stored in the Hadoop filesystem. The document file is stored using Apache Avro, which provides a high-performance and dynamic serialization layer. Avro takes a record definition and enables serialization/deserialization based on it. The record structure, in this case, is for a document and is defined as follows:

```
{"namespace": "storm.cookbook",
 "type": "record",
 "name": "Document",
 "fields": [
     {"name": "docid", "type": "string"},
     {"name": "time",  "type": "long"},
     {"name": "line", "type": "string"}
 ]
}
```

Both the `stop` words and documents are fed through an ETL function that emits a clean set of words that have been filtered. The words are derived by splitting the `line` field using a regular expression:

```
(defmapcatop split [line]
    (s/split line #"[\[\]\\\(\),.)\s]+"))
```

The ETL function is also a query, which serves as a source for our downstream queries, and defines the `[?doc-id ?time ?word]` output fields.

The output tap, or sink, is based on the Cassandra scheme. A query defines predicate logic, not the source and destination of data. The sink ensures that the outputs of our queries are sent to Cassandra. The `?-` macro executes a query, and it is only at execution time that a query is bound to its source and destination, again allowing for extreme levels of composition. The following, therefore, executes the TF query and outputs to Cassandra:

```
(?- (create-tf-tap cassandra-ip)
        (TF src))
```

There's more...

The Avro test data was created using the test data from the Cascading tutorial at `http://www.cascading.org/2012/07/31/cascading-for-the-impatient-part-5/`. Within this tutorial is the `rain.txt` tab-separated data file. A new column was created called `time` that holds the Unix epoc time in milliseconds. The updated text file was then processed using some basic Java code that leverages Avro:

```
Schema schema = Schema.parse(SandboxMain.class.getResourceAsStream("/
document.avsc"));
    File file = new File("document.avro");
    DatumWriter<GenericRecord> datumWriter = new GenericDatumWriter<
                                          GenericRecord>(schema);
    DataFileWriter<GenericRecord> dataFileWriter =
                    new DataFileWriter<GenericRecord>(datumWriter);
    dataFileWriter.create(schema, file);
    BufferedReader reader = new BufferedReader(new
    InputStreamReader(SandboxMain.class.getResourceAsStream(
                                      "/rain.txt")));
    String line = null;

    try {
        while ((line = reader.readLine()) != null) {
            String[] tokens = line.split("\t");
            GenericRecord docEntry = new
                                  GenericData.Record(schema);
            docEntry.put("docid", tokens[0]);
            docEntry.put("time", Long.parseLong(tokens[1]));
            docEntry.put("line", tokens[2]);
            dataFileWriter.append(docEntry);
        }
    } catch (IOException e) {
        e.printStackTrace();
    }
    dataFileWriter.close();
```

Persisting documents from Storm

In the previous recipe, we looked at deriving precomputed views of our data taking some immutable data as the source. In that recipe, we used statically created data. In an operational system, we need Storm to store the immutable data into Hadoop so that it can be used in any preprocessing that is required.

How to do it...

As each tuple is processed in Storm, we must generate an Avro record based on the document record definition and append it to the data file within the Hadoop filesystem.

We must create a Trident function that takes each document tuple and stores the associated Avro record.

1. Within the `tfidf-topology` project created in *Chapter 3, Calculating Term Importance with Trident*, inside the `storm.cookbook.tfidf.function` package, create a new class named `PersistDocumentFunction` that extends `BaseFunction`. Within the `prepare` function, initialize the Avro schema and document writer:

```
public void prepare(Map conf, TridentOperationContext context) {
       try {
           String path = (String) conf.get("DOCUMENT_PATH");
           schema = Schema.parse(PersistDocumentFunction.class
                 .getResourceAsStream("/document.avsc"));
           File file = new File(path);
           DatumWriter<GenericRecord> datumWriter = new GenericDatum
                                       Writer<GenericRecord>(schema);
           dataFileWriter = new DataFileWriter<GenericRecord>(
                                                   datumWriter);
           if(file.exists())
              dataFileWriter.appendTo(file);
           else
              dataFileWriter.create(schema, file);
       } catch (IOException e) {
          throw new RuntimeException(e);
       }

    }
```

2. As each tuple is received, coerce it into an Avro record and add it to the file:

```
public void execute(TridentTuple tuple, TridentCollector
collector) {
       GenericRecord docEntry = new GenericData.Record(schema);
       docEntry.put("docid", tuple.getStringByField("documentId"));
       docEntry.put("time", Time.currentTimeMillis());
       docEntry.put("line", tuple.getStringByField("document"));
       try {
          dataFileWriter.append(docEntry);
          dataFileWriter.flush();
       } catch (IOException e) {
```

```
                    LOG.error("Error writing to document record: " + e);
                    throw new RuntimeException(e);
            }

        }
```

3. Next, edit the `TermTopology.build` topology and add the function to the
    document stream:

    ```
    documentStream.each(new Fields("documentId","document"),
                   new PersistDocumentFunction(), new Fields());
    ```

4. Finally, include the document path into the topology configuration:

    ```
    conf.put("DOCUMENT_PATH", "document.avro");
    ```

How it works...

There are various logical streams within the topology, and certainly the input for the topology
is not in the appropriate state for the recipes in this chapter containing only URLs. We
therefore need to select the correct stream from which to consume tuples, coerce these into
Avro records, and serialize them into a file.

The previous recipe will then periodically consume this file. Within the context of the topology
definition, include the following code:

```
Stream documentStream = getUrlStream(topology, spout)
            .each(new Fields("url"),
                new DocumentFetchFunction(mimeTypes),
                new Fields("document", "documentId", "source"));

    documentStream.each(new Fields("documentId","document"),
                new PersistDocumentFunction(), new Fields());
```

The function should consume tuples from the document stream whose tuples are populated
with already fetched documents.

Integrating the batch and real-time views

The final step to complete the big data architecture is largely complete already and is
surprisingly simple, as is the case with all good functional style designs.

How to do it...

This recipe involves simply extending the existing TF-IDF DRPC query that we defined in *Chapter 4, Distributed Remote Procedure Calls*. We need three new state sources that represents the D, DF, and TF values computed in the Batch layer. We will combine the values from these states with the existing state before performing the final TF-IDF calculation.

1. Start from the inside out by creating the combination function called `BatchCombiner` within the `storm.cookbook.tfidf.function` package and implement the logic to combine two versions of the same state. One version should be from the current hour, and the other from all the data prior to the current hour:

```
public void execute(TridentTuple tuple, TridentCollector
collector) {
    try {
      double d_rt = (double) tuple.getLongByField("d_rt");
      double df_rt = (double) tuple.getLongByField("df_rt");
      double tf_rt = (double) tuple.getLongByField("tf_rt");

      double d_batch = (double) tuple.getLongByField("d_batch");
      double df_batch = (double) tuple.getLongByField("df_batch");
      double tf_batch = (double) tuple.getLongByField("tf_batch");

      collector.emit(new Values(tf_rt + tf_batch, d_rt +
                    d_batch, df_rt + df_batch));
    } catch (Exception e) {
    }

  }
```

2. Add the state to the topology by adding these calls to the `addTFIDFQueryStream` function:

```
TridentState batchDfState = topology.newStaticState(
                    getBatchStateFactory("df"));
TridentState batchDState = topology.newStaticState(
                    getBatchStateFactory("d"));
TridentState batchTfState = topology.newStaticState(
                    getBatchStateFactory("tf"));
```

3. This is supported by the static utility function:

```
private static StateFactory getBatchStateFactory(String rowKey) {
      CassandraState.Options options = new CassandraState.
Options();
      options.keyspace = "storm";
      options.columnFamily = "tfidfbatch";
```

```
        options.rowKey = rowKey;
        return CassandraState.nonTransactional("localhost",
options);
    }
```

 Within a cluster deployment of Cassandra, simply replace the word `localhost` with a list of seed node IP addresses. Seed nodes are simply Cassandra nodes, which, when appropriately configured, will know about their peers in the cluster. For more information on Cassandra, please see the online documentation at `http://wiki.apache.org/cassandra/GettingStarted`.

4. Finally, edit the existing DRPC query to reflect the added state and combiner function:

```
topology.newDRPCStream("tfidfQuery",drpc)
            .each(new Fields("args"),
            new SplitAndProjectToFields(),
            new Fields("documentId", "term"))
            .each(new Fields(),
            new StaticSourceFunction("twitter"),
            new Fields("source")).stateQuery(tfState,
            new Fields("documentId", "term"),
            new MapGet(), new Fields("tf_rt"))
            .stateQuery(dfState,new Fields("term"),
            new MapGet(), new Fields("df_rt"))
            .stateQuery(dState,new Fields("source"),
            new MapGet(), new Fields("d_rt"))
            .stateQuery(batchTfState,
            new Fields("documentId", "term"),
            new MapGet(), new Fields("tf_batch"))
            .stateQuery(batchDfState,new Fields("term"),
            new MapGet(), new Fields("df_batch"))
            .stateQuery(batchDState,new Fields("source"),
            new MapGet(), new Fields("d_batch"))
            .each(new Fields("tf_rt","df_rt",
            "d_rt","tf_batch","df_batch","d_batch"), new
            BatchCombiner(), new Fields("tf","d","df"))
            .each(new Fields("term","documentId","tf","d",
            "df"), new TfidfExpression(),
            new Fields("tfidf"))
            .each(new Fields("tfidf"), new FilterNull())
            .project(new Fields("documentId",
                    "term","tfidf"));
```

How it works...

We have covered a huge amount of ground to get to this point. We have implemented an entire real-time, big data architecture that is fault-tolerant, scalable, and reliable using purely open source technologies. It is therefore useful at this point to recap the journey we have taken to the point, ending back where we are now:

- ▶ We learned how to implement a Trident topology and define a stream data pipeline. This data pipeline defines predicates that not only act on tuples but also on persistent, mutable states.

- ▶ Using this pipeline, we implemented the TF-IDF algorithm.

- ▶ We separated out the preprocessing stage of the data pipeline from the "at time" stage of the pipeline. We achieved this by implementing a portion of the pipeline in a DRPC stream that is only invoked at "at time".

- ▶ We then added the concept of time windows to the topology. This allowed us to segment the state into time-window buckets. We chose hours as a convenient segmentation.

- ▶ We learned how to test a time-dependent topology using the Clojure testing API.

- ▶ Then, in this chapter, we implemented the immutable state and the batch computation.

- ▶ Finally, we combined the batch-computed view with the mutable state to provide a complete solution.

The following flow diagram illustrates the entire process:

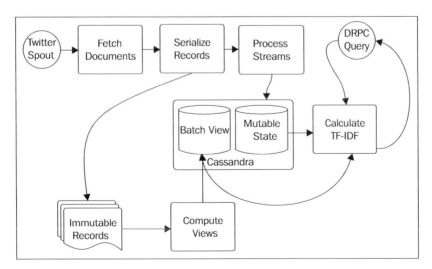

With the high-level picture in place, the final DRPC query stream becomes easier to understand. The stream effectively implements the following steps:

- ▶ `.each(SplitAndProjectToFields)`: This splits the input arguments from the query and projects them out into separate fields in the tuple

- ▶ `.each(StaticSourceFunction)`: This adds a static value to the stream, which will be required later

- ▶ `.stateQuery(tfState)`: This queries the state of the `tf` value for the current hour based on the document ID and term and outputs `tf_rt`

- ▶ `.stateQuery(dState)`: This queries the state of the `d` value for the current hour based on the static source value and outputs `d_rt`

- ▶ `.stateQuery(dfState)`: This queries the state of the `df` value for the current hour based on the term and outputs `df_rt`

- ▶ `.stateQuery(tfBatchState)`: This queries the state of the `tf` value for all previous hours based on the document ID and term and outputs `tf_batch`

- ▶ `.stateQuery(dBatchState)`: This queries the state of the `d` value for all previous hours based on the static source value and outputs `d_batch`

- ▶ `.stateQuery(dfBatchState)`: This queries the state of the `df` value for all previous hours based on the term and outputs `df_batch`

- ▶ `.each(BatchCombiner)`: This combines the separate `_rt` and `_batch` fields into a single set of values

- ▶ `.each(TfidfExpression)`: This calculates the TF-IDF final value

- ▶ `.project`: This projects just the fields we require in the output

A key to understanding this is that in each stage in this process, the tuple is simply receiving new values and each function is simply adding new named values to the tuple. The state queries are doing the same based on existing fields within the tuple. Finally, we end up with a very "wide" tuple that we trim down before returning the final result.

7

Real-time Machine Learning

In this chapter, we will cover:

- ▶ Implementing a transactional topology
- ▶ Creating a Random Forest classification model using R
- ▶ Operational classification of transactional streams using Random Forest
- ▶ Creating an association rules model in R
- ▶ Creating a recommendation engine
- ▶ Real-time online machine learning

Introduction

We have explored how Storm fits into a Big Data architecture as the real-time layer. A key use case for Big Data solutions involves the enabling of **data science**. We have seen some basic data science already through the implementation of some basic analysis of term frequencies, both in real time and batch. When analyzing data, there are both operational and insights components to the process. The operational component is the one we have explored already in great detail using Storm—the ability to process data streams and identify important terms. Insights involve aggregated views of large datasets such that they provide some higher-level insight, and is typically an offline activity. It answers the following questions:

- ▶ Which market segment is the most effective?
- ▶ How can I engage more effectively with my customer?
- ▶ What is my current financial position?

Insights are, therefore, associated with traditional **Management Information Systems** (**MIS**); however, systems that deliver insights are changing with the proliferation of Big Data technology.

Both operationally and in terms of insights, we have only explored data analysis and data science in terms of a single temporal dimension—the past. This chapter concerns itself with the future. Increasingly, business is dependent on knowing what to expect before it happens. This branch of data science is known by many names: machine learning, predictive analytics, and artificial intelligence. Within this text, the terms machine learning and predictive analytics will be used interchangeably. There are many use cases for machine learning, and some of them are as follows:

▸ Product recommendation

▸ Customer churn prediction

▸ Fraud detection and prevention

▸ Credit and risk management

▸ Governance and control

Within predictive analytics, one still needs to distinguish between operational analytics and insights. This chapter will largely focus on the operational aspects, given that Storm is a platform ideally suited for this purpose; however, areas where insights are involved will also be identified.

A final classification that is important at this stage is the high-level families of predictive models and algorithms. At a high level, two families exist, namely supervised and unsupervised. The distinction between these two refers to the way in which the model is trained or built. Which can either be done through training data that contains both features and known target values; or the models can be built without targets, leaving the discovery of any targets purely to the algorithm.

This distinction deserves more explanation; however, it must be noted that this book does not aim to present a complete overview of machine learning, rather simply introduce how to implement such techniques using Storm. With that goal in mind, some concepts will be explained to a reasonable level of detail, some will be grossly over simplified, and some will be ignored entirely. Machine learning is an extremely large and complex area, and it is highly recommended that the reader explores the topic in greater detail using one of the many online resources available to them.

Returning to supervised learning, we shall start with some terminology. For a given dataset, specifically, for each datum within a dataset, there exist certain classes of fields:

▸ **Features**: This class refers to properties of the datum, which typically are the properties that of interest and hopefully contain some inherent predictive ability when viewed with the correct lens.

▸ **Labels**: This class refers to some known outcome that is relative to the given set of features.

▶ **Identifier**: This class refers to a field that can identify the particular datum within the dataset.

For a better understanding of these terms, those with any relational database experience, can think about these classes in terms of a single table with rows and columns. These terms describe the types of columns one would expect in a dataset that are to be used for training a supervised learning algorithm. Therefore, while building a model, each datum is a row in that table. By way of an example, suppose that you had an audit dataset with the following columns:

▶ ID

▶ Age

▶ Employment status

▶ Education

▶ Marital status

▶ Occupation

▶ Income

▶ Gender

▶ Risk classification

Age, Employment status, Education, Marital status, Occupation, Income, and Gender are the features of this dataset. ID would be the identifier and the Risk classification column would be the target field (often referred to as the label). By including the target field, we are asking an algorithm to find some relationships within the features that will result in a given outcome. The algorithm is therefore said to be supervised.

When no target is given, the algorithm is said to be unsupervised in nature, in that, it needs to find relationships in the data without this guiding data. Random Forest is an example of a supervised model, whereas K-Means is an example of an unsupervised model.

The fundamental assumption built into machine learning is that things that occurred in the past will happen in similar ways in the future. Various machine learning algorithms attempt to extract the underlying concepts inherent in the featured set of data, and then use these concepts in predicting future events of a similar kind. Of course, this assumption is invalidated entirely through novel data; however, the vast majority of data isn't novel.

This chapter demonstrates the implementation of such techniques on Storm, and the concepts that have been introduced extremely briefly here will be explained further as and when appropriate.

There are three approaches to implementing machine learning within Storm. We will explore all the three (Storm-Pattern, Storm-R, and Trident-ML) approaches, but first, let's lay a basis for achieving exactly-once semantics.

Implementing a transactional topology

In the previous chapters, we have concerned ourselves with data that was not "transactional" in nature, not in the way we typically think of things such as financial transactions. As a result, one can potentially tolerate system failure because there is no direct monetary implication to each transaction that may be affected by any failure cases, especially given that transactional schematics come with a cost, both in performance and storage. The recipes in this chapter deal with scoring transactions that require transactional schematics, and it is therefore relevant to understand how to achieve exactly-once schematics with Storm at this stage.

 The transactional schematics of Storm, like most aspects of Storm, are excellently documented on the project's wiki. The transactional logic is presented here as a matter of convenience and completeness, but the reader is encouraged to read the source of this information at `https://github.com/nathanmarz/storm/wiki/Trident-state`.

Trident's support for exactly-once schematics requires specific implementations of spouts and state. When failures occur, tuples will be replayed. This brings up a problem when doing state updates (or anything with side effects)—you have no idea if you've ever successfully updated the state based on this tuple before. The state, therefore, needs to be fundamentally idempotent. In order to achieve this, you use the following properties of Storm:

- Tuples are processed as small batches.
- Each batch of tuples is given a unique ID called the **transaction ID** (**txid**). If the batch is replayed, it is given the exact same txid.
- State updates are ordered among batches; that is, the state updates for batch 2 won't be applied until the state updates for batch 1 have succeeded.

Given these properties, and storing a little extra state, it is possible to ensure that state updates are truly idempotent in the face of failures and retries.

The key to implementing these properties is the spout. The spout must follow a specific set of rules:

- Batches for a given txid are always the same. Replays of batches for a txid will extract the same set of tuples as the first time that batch was emitted for that txid.
- There's no overlap between the batches of tuples (tuples are in one batch or another, never multiple).
- Every tuple is in a batch.

Finally, the transaction ID is stored atomically with the value in the underlying Trident state. Using this transaction ID, Trident is can detect if a given update is a duplicate of a previous update involving this batch and can decide whether to skip or apply this update. The logic of including the transaction ID is handled entirely by Trident and its state implementations and works regardless of the underlying persistence.

Getting ready

Before we get started, we need to install a message broker that more readily supports the transactional logic inherent in Storm's Trident, specifically Apache Kafka. **Kafka** is a distributed publish-subscribe messaging system. According to the Kafka website (`http://kafka.apache.org/`), it is designed to support the following:

▶ Persistent messaging with O(1) disk structures that provide constant time performance even with many TB of stored messages.

▶ High-throughput is supported; even with very modest hardware, Kafka can support hundreds of thousands of messages per second.

▶ Explicit support for partitioning messages over Kafka servers and distributing consumption over a cluster of consumer machines while maintaining per-partition ordering semantics.

In order to install Kafka, download the source packages from the website for Version 0.7.2. Once the download is complete, install **Scala Build Tool** (**sbt**), then unpack and build the Kafka server by executing the following command:

```
sudo apt-get install sbt

tar xzf kafka-0.7.2-incubating-src.tgz

cd kafka-0.7.2-incubating-src

./sbt update

./sbt package
```

The default installation of Kafka sets the number of partitions to 1, which isn't a practical value. So, start by editing the `server.properties` file under `config` and setting the value of `num.partitions` to 2.

With Kafka installed, open up three separate terminal instances within the `kafka` directory. Within the first terminal, execute the following command:

```
bin/zookeeper-server-start.sh config/zookeeper.properties
```

Then, from within the second terminal, execute the following command:

```
bin/kafka-server-start.sh config/server.properties
```

You now have a functioning Kafka server. Note that your Zookeeper and Kafka instance are executing in separate terminals. Your third terminal will be used to interact with Kafka topics. To test your installation, let's publish some messages. In the third terminal instance, execute the following command:

```
bin/kafka-console-producer.sh --zookeeper localhost:2181 --topic test
```

Once the initialization sequence is complete, you will be able to type text; each line you type will publish that text to the "test" topic. Enter a few lines and then escape the application by using *Ctrl + C*. Finally, verify that the messages can be read; to do this, type the following command into the terminal:

```
bin/kafka-console-consumer.sh --zookeeper localhost:2181 --topic test
--from-beginning
```

This application should display all of your previously created messages. You can use *Ctrl + C* to quit this application, but note that we will be shortly using this subscriber utility for testing.

How to do it...

We will now implement an extremely basic transactional topology. This will illustrate how transactional semantics are achieved in Storm. In order to fully illustrate this, we will create the topology and test and understand the resulting state, but we will also create some forced errors in order to check whether the failure and recovery cases are working. This will give you a clear understanding of how the transactional elements hang together and where to start debugging should you encounter errors.

1. Start by creating a Storm project that includes the following dependencies in the POM file:

```xml
<dependency>
    <groupId>storm</groupId>
    <artifactId>storm-kafka</artifactId>
    <version>0.9.0-wip16a-scala292</version>
    <exclusions>
        <exclusion>
            <artifactId>storm</artifactId>
            <groupId>storm</groupId>
        </exclusion>
    </exclusions>
</dependency>
<dependency>
    <groupId>org.slf4j</groupId>
    <artifactId>slf4j-log4j12</artifactId>
    <version>1.6.1</version>
</dependency>
<dependency>
    <groupId>trident-cassandra</groupId>
    <artifactId>trident-cassandra</artifactId>
    <version>0.0.1-bucketwip1</version>
    <exclusions>
        <exclusion>
            <artifactId>storm</artifactId>
```

```
            <groupId>storm</groupId>
        </exclusion>
    </exclusions>
</dependency>
```

2. Import your project into Eclipse, create a new main class named `TransactionalTopology`, and then create the basic main method implementation:

```
Config conf = new Config();
    conf.setDebug(true);

    conf.setMaxTaskParallelism(3);

    LocalCluster cluster = new LocalCluster();
cluster.submitTopology("transactional-topology",
                    conf,makeTopology().build());

    Thread.sleep(100000);

    cluster.shutdown();
```

3. Then, define a really simple topology in the `makeTopology()` method:

```
TridentTopology topology = new TridentTopology();

    TridentKafkaConfig spoutConfig = new TridentKafkaConfig(
                        StaticHosts.fromHostString(
                        Arrays.asList(new String[] {
                        "localhost" }), 2), "test");

    topology.newStream("kafka", new TransactionalTridentKafkaSpout(
                    spoutConfig))
        .each(new Fields("bytes"), new DebugBytes(), new
            Fields("text"))
        .groupBy(new Fields("text"))
        .persistentAggregate(getBatchStateFactory("test"), new
                        Count(), new Fields("count"));

    return topology;
```

4. In order to complete the topology definition, you must implement the `DebugBytes` Trident function. Trident ships with a built-in `Debug` function, but here we need a specialized equivalent that prints out the message contents and generates periodic errors. To implement this, simply maintain a member-level count and throw exceptions based on modulus tests within the `execute` method:

```
count++;
    if(count % 2 == 0){
        throw new RuntimeException("Testing");
```

```
        }
    String text = new String(tuple.getBinary(0));
        System.out.println(name + text);
        collector.emit(new Values(text));
```

5. This is the complete implementation. So, we can simply expect the topology to print our messages, group them by content, and store a count against content in a Cassandra column family. Before we test the topology, you need to create the Cassandra column family; execute the following commands in the Cassandra-cli to do so:

```
create keyspace test
    with strategy_options = [{replication_factor:1}]
    and placement_strategy = 'org.apache.cassandra.locator.
                            SimpleStrategy';


use test;
create column family transactional
    with comparator = AsciiType
    and default_validation_class = 'UTF8Type'
    and key_validation_class = 'UTF8Type';
```

6. You can now test the topology by starting it directly from Eclipse by navigating to **Run As | Java Application**. Once the topology is initialized, switch back to your third Kafka terminal and run the following command to start the message producer:

```
bin/kafka-console-producer.sh --zookeeper localhost:2181 --topic
test
```

7. Using this interface, publish a single message. Then, take note of the Storm logs, which should be clear. Also take note of the value in the Cassandra column family, which you can do by the following Cassandra-cli instructions:

```
use test;
```
```
list transactional;
```

Note that the value stored in Cassandra contains more than just your intended count of 1.

8. Now, switch back to the terminal and enter a second message. At this point, your topology should throw an exception and terminate. Validate that this has occurred, and also validate that the stored count is still 1.

You have effectively simulated a failure during transaction processing. The expected behavior now is that you can start up the topology again, the message should now be processed, and the count in Cassandra should be updated to 2. To test this, simply run the topology again in local mode from Eclipse.

9. When you execute this , you will notice that the message does not get replayed into the topology, and the count remains at 1 until you publish a third message. This means that the message was effectively lost as a result of the failure case. This is obviously what we are trying to prevent; in order to fix the issue, add the following lines of code to your main method:

```
conf.put(Config.STORM_ZOOKEEPER_SERVERS, Arrays.asList(new
String[]{"127.0.0.1"}));
conf.put(Config.STORM_ZOOKEEPER_PORT, 2181);
conf.put(Config.STORM_ZOOKEEPER_ROOT, "/storm");
```

10. You can now re-run the same test, you will find that after the failure, the topology does replay the message and the count is updated as expected.

How it works...

We saw many elements coming together in order to provide the exactly-once semantics that we finally witnessed during our tests. Let's unpack each element at play.

Firstly, the Kafka spout, which is a prebuilt module from the `storm-contrib` project, already implements the required set of logic to be a transactional compliant spout. We configured the spout using the following lines of code:

```
TridentKafkaConfig spoutConfig = new TridentKafkaConfig(
                          StaticHosts.fromHostString(
                          Arrays.asList(new String[] {
                          localhost" }), 2), "test");
```

This configuration tells Kafka where to find the Kafka nodes. In this case, we only have a single node on localhost; however, in a larger deployment, we would supply a list of actual Kafka nodes. We also specify the number of partitions and the name of the topic to subscribe to. We then create an instance of a transactional spout as the spout for the only stream in our topology. This is all that is required to implement a transactional Kafka spout. Many other transactional spouts exist within the `storm-contrib` project; however, if your broker isn't currently supported, using the existing `storm-contrib` code as a starting point would be the best approach to implementing a new spout.

Secondly, we have seen the transactional state in the Cassandra-backed Trident state. Trident adds some transaction IS state to the `state` element in the underlying data store on our behalf. It then also uses this state to safely replay the message and update the state. In order to use the transactional state, ensure that you create your Cassandra state using the transactional utility method.

Finally, we managed to create failure cases, which weren't dealt with correctly without adding some additional configurations for the topology. The properties in question effectively tell Storm where to find a running Zookeeper instance:

```
conf.put(Config.STORM_ZOOKEEPER_SERVERS, Arrays.asList(new String[]
{"127.0.0.1"}));
conf.put(Config.STORM_ZOOKEEPER_PORT, 2181);
conf.put(Config.STORM_ZOOKEEPER_ROOT, "/storm");
```

This fixes the problem, because Storm stores an additional bit of state in Zookeeper, which allows Storm to enforce strong ordering between batches. This is key, Trident allows for parallel processing of batches; however, they always commit in order. This capability is enabled by maintaining a batch-tracking state inside zookeeper. Within a standard deployment, there is no need to tell Storm where to find Zookeeper; however, in the local mode, there is no Zookeeper instance running, thus the requirement for this configuration.

Creating a Random Forest classification model using R

As mentioned in the introduction to the chapter, three approaches to machine learning within Storm will be presented. It is important to understand when to use each approach. This choice starts by understanding what machine learning approach and algorithm you would like to use: online or batch-based. Remember that, for machine learning, *online* and *batch* refers to the way in which the model is trained. This distinction does not imply any particular underlying engineering approach to achieve either the batch or online modes. A batch model can be built in a real-time software platform, and conversely, an online model can be built as part of a batch software process. It is important to understand this distinction between the engineering aspect and the machine learning aspect.

If you would like to explore this concept in more depth, please read the following overview of neural networks in which the distinction is explored in more detail: http://www.webpages. ttu.edu/dleverin/neural_network/neural_networks.html.

Once you have chosen your algorithm approach, you can use the following guidelines to choose the correct approach within Storm:

► **Storm-Pattern**: Pattern is a port of the Cascading/Pattern project. It aims to support the operational deployment of all of the most common models, imported via PMML. This is the preferred approach when batch training a model. The model can then be used to score a stream of data. It is preferred because of the following reasons:

  ❑ It achieves the highest performance through native scoring implementations

  ❑ PMML is a well-supported standard for exchanging models, and you can build your model using a wide range of solutions, from R to SAS and anything in between.

- ▶ **Storm-R**: The R integration is useful when a given model isn't yet supported by Storm-Pattern but is supported by R (R supports a massive range of models). The model can then be operationalized into Storm using the Storm-R integration with very little effort. However, this method isn't preferred because of the performance characteristics of R and the coupling to R as a technology. In many environments R isn't used at all.

- ▶ **Trident-ML**: This is an excellent implementation of many of the most common algorithms that support online learning. This is the approach to use if you are needing to implement an online learning mode.

With this framework in place, we can proceed to the first use case, which is batch-building a model and exporting it to be operationalized later using Storm-Pattern.

Getting ready

To get started, you need to download the latest version of R from `http://www.r-project.org/`. It is also recommended that you download RStudio, which is an excellent open source Integrated Development Environment (IDE) for R from `http://www.rstudio.com/`. Once you have installed R and RStudio, open R Studio and you should be presented with a view similar to the following screenshot:

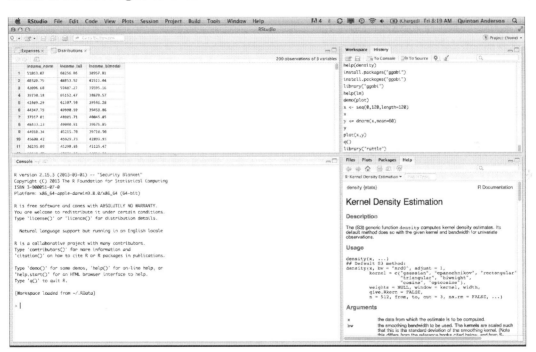

While a comprehensive overview of R is well outside of the scope of this book, a quick overview is relevant and useful. The RStudio environment consists of the following four areas:

▶ Data view, docked to the top-left corner, allows you to view datasets within the workspace.

▶ The history, docked to the top-right corner, allows you to view all your previous commands. This dock position also contains all the variables that are currently stored in the workspace and available as variables within the REPL.

▶ The REPL is docked to the bottom-left corner and is the main work area where you will input code and receive feedback.

▶ Finally, the bottom-right dock location contains a help view and the plots that we have generated as part of the any statistical analysis that we perform within the REPL.

R has many useful functions to help the user, such as `help([function name])`, which will display comprehensive help for the specified command. You can also search the R archives and packages for particular terms or functions by simply typing `??[Search Criteria]`.

For this recipe, we are going to require two R packages, namely `pmml` and `randomForest`. In order to install them, enter the following commands in the REPL:

```
install.packages("pmml")
install.packages("randomForest")
```

RStudio will prompt you to choose a mirror and then install the required packages.

Finally, you will need the dataset, which you can download from: `https://bitbucket.org/qanderson/rf-topology/raw/ac1e5ff8117ae773be4c29c8c5b63f17c51a6654/orders.tsv`.

How to do it...

Using the `randomForest` package, we will now build a Random Forest model and then export it using PMML.

1. Start by loading the required libraries. In the REPL, enter the following commands:

```
library(pmml)
library(randomForest)
```

2. Then, load the required data as follows:

```
dat_folder <- '.'
data <- read.table(file="orders.tsv", sep="\t", quote="",
na.strings="NULL", header=TRUE, encoding="UTF8")

dim(data)
head(data)
```

3. Next, you need to split the data into training and testing datasets as described in the followingcommand line:

```
set.seed(71)
split_ratio <- 2/10
split <- round(dim(data)[1] * split_ratio)

data_tests <- data[1:split,]
dim(data_tests)
print(table(data_tests[,"label"]))

data_train <- data[(split + 1):dim(data)[1],]
i <- colnames(data_train) == "order_id"
j <- 1:length(i)
data_train <- data_train[,-j[i]]
dim(data_train)
```

4. You then need to train the Random Forest model as described here:

```
f <- as.formula("as.factor(label) ~ .")
fit <- randomForest(f, data_train, ntree=500)
```

5. You can then test the model by entering the following commands and inspecting the resulting confusion matrix:

```
print(fit$importance)
print(fit)

predicted <- predict(fit, data)
data$predict <- predicted
confuse <- table(pred = predicted, true = data[,1])
print(confuse)
```

The confusion matrix allows you to inspect the performance of the model against the **Out Of Bag (OOB)** data.

6. Finally, export the model using PMML as follows:

```
saveXML(pmml(fit), file="random_forest.xml", sep="/")
```

How it works...

The following diagram illustrates the basic process involved in building a model:

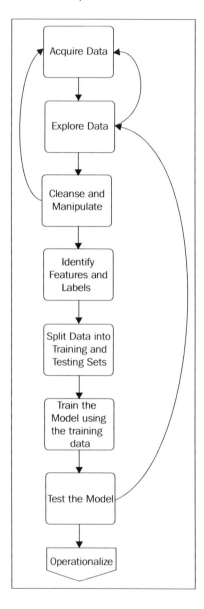

The key element to understand is that the process of model building is highly iterative and interactive. RStudio is a powerful tool to help you with this process. The code that you entered will build you an excellent model based on a prebuilt and clean dataset that was prepared for training purposes. When applied to real-world datasets, the process is always far more incremental and difficult, often including many other statistical techniques in order to analyze and manipulate the data. Furthermore, depending on the size of the dataset, you may need to apply other approaches to test the model effectively. Again, these topics are all subjects of entire books in their own right, and they are mentioned here in order to draw your attention to them; further reading is required if you would like to build models effectively in the real world.

The Random Forest is an extremely useful tool, especially for those starting out in machine learning. It is an ensemble method that can be used for either regression or classification tasks. Random Forest works by growing a multitude of decision trees, and a variation between the trees is introduced by projecting the training data into a randomly chosen subspace before fitting each tree. Essentially, each tree is trained on a bootstrapped sample of the original dataset, and each time a leaf is split, only a randomly chosen subset of the dimensions are considered for splitting. This ensures that the key underlying concepts that are inherent in the data are chosen, making for far more accurate OOB test results than a standard decision tree.

A Random Forest actually goes far beyond what I have described here; however, for our purposes, this will suffice, as all the complexity has been abstracted away within the R packages.

Good analysis is underpinned by an excellent understanding of the data; the exploring phase is essential, and you should spend much time getting to know your dataset. Let's take a quick look at our particular dataset. In RStudio, execute the following commands:

```
orders <- read.delim("~/workspace/rf-topology/orders.tsv")

View(orders)

contents(orders)

summary(orders)
```

These commands should give you three critical outputs to help you to start understanding the data. Firstly, you will get a view of the data in a table to the top-left of the display. Secondly, you will get a summary of the fields in the dataset and their types, and it should look something like the following command line:

```
Data frame:orders    1000 observations and 12 variables    Maximum # NAs:0
```

	Levels	Storage
label		integer
v0		double
v1		double
v2		double

```
v3                double
v4                double
v5                double
v6                double
v7                double
v8                double
v9                double
order_id   1000 integer


+--------+-----------------------------------------------------------
-------------------------------------------+
|Variable|Levels
|
+--------+-----------------------------------------------------------
-------------------------------------------+
|order_id|f46f652b,f4702b0f,f4702d99,f47030e8,f47034dc,f47037e8,f4703a35,
f4703c6e,f4703e9e,f47040d9,f4704300,f470453a|
|        |f4704773,f470497a,f4704bfd,f4704e0c,f4705017,f4705214,f470541c,
f470560f,f4705817,f4705a1e,f4705c1e,f4705e1c|
```

Our dataset has 12 fields, a label, an order ID, and the remaining 10 fields (v0 to v9, all of type double). The output also tells us that we have 1000 observations or rows. The contents function also discovers that the order ID is a discrete set of values and tries to list them for us; the terminology within R refers to these discrete values as levels. In this example, the Levels output isn't particularly useful, but there are many cases where it is. For this example, looking at the data values in the data explorer and contents output, we can be quite certain that fields v0 to v9 are our features, and we have a label and an identifier, which appears to be some portion of a UUID or similar concept.

Finally, you will get a summary of the dataset at a field level that should look similar to the following screenshot:

```
        label              v0                 v1                 v2
 Min.   :0.000     Min.   :-1.980     Min.   :-1.560     Min.   :-1.550
 1st Qu.:0.000     1st Qu.: 0.690     1st Qu.: 0.720     1st Qu.: 0.690
 Median :0.000     Median : 1.270     Median : 1.290     Median : 1.280
 Mean   :0.209     Mean   : 1.068     Mean   : 1.117     Mean   : 1.091
 3rd Qu.:0.000     3rd Qu.: 1.550     3rd Qu.: 1.570     3rd Qu.: 1.560
 Max.   :1.000     Max.   : 2.450     Max.   : 2.360     Max.   : 2.440

        v3                 v4                 v5                 v6
 Min.   :-2.300    Min.   :-1.660     Min.   :-2.080     Min.   :-2.130
 1st Qu.: 0.680    1st Qu.: 0.630     1st Qu.: 0.680     1st Qu.: 0.710
 Median : 1.280    Median : 1.270     Median : 1.280     Median : 1.280
 Mean   : 1.072    Mean   : 1.053     Mean   : 1.075     Mean   : 1.104
 3rd Qu.: 1.560    3rd Qu.: 1.550     3rd Qu.: 1.550     3rd Qu.: 1.570
 Max.   : 2.230    Max.   : 2.200     Max.   : 2.250     Max.   : 2.220

        v7                 v8                 v9                order_id
 Min.   :-1.490    Min.   :-1.900     Min.   :-1.580     f46f652b:   1
 1st Qu.: 0.700    1st Qu.: 0.710     1st Qu.: 0.700     f4702b0f:   1
 Median : 1.275    Median : 1.280     Median : 1.270     f4702d99:   1
 Mean   : 1.074    Mean   : 1.087     Mean   : 1.083     f47030e8:   1
 3rd Qu.: 1.560    3rd Qu.: 1.540     3rd Qu.: 1.560     f47034dc:   1
 Max.   : 2.330    Max.   : 2.230     Max.   : 2.220     f47037e8:   1
                                                         (Other) :994
```

The importance of these outputs is that you can start to understand the type of data that you have within your feature fields: the range, median, and mean of each.

With this clearer understanding of the data in hand, you may practically need to filter, enrich, or clean the data as required.

In this recipe, a dataset was provided that did not require such cleansing; therefore, you moved directly on to building the model. The steps between getting the data and building the model involved segmenting the data into training set and testing set are given as follows:

```
set.seed(71)
split_ratio <- 2/10
split <- round(dim(data)[1] * split_ratio)


data_tests <- data[1:split,]
dim(data_tests)
print(table(data_tests[,"label"]))


data_train <- data[(split + 1):dim(data)[1],]
i <- colnames(data_train) == "order_id"
j <- 1:length(i)
data_train <- data_train[,-j[i]]
dim(data_train)
```

This step is vital in order to evaluate the model. You can't validate the model using data that it has already "seen", so segmenting the original dataset allows us to keep a portion of the data aside for evaluating the model later, which can be achieved through the following commands:

```
predicted <- predict(fit, data)
data$predict <- predicted
confuse <- table(pred = predicted, true = data[,1])
print(confuse)
```

There's more...

The **Predictive Model Markup Language** (**PMML**) is an XML-based markup language developed by the **Data Mining Group** (**DMG**) to provide a way for applications to define models related to predictive analytics and data mining, and to share those models between PMML-compliant applications.

The PMML standard creates an excellent way to decouple the system that generates the model from the system that provides the operational scoring. This is architecturally significant because systems such as R, SAS, and Weka are excellent at performing analytics, but are not well-suited to use in operational settings. Furthermore, scoring is often required within the context of a larger operational system, and therefore coupling analytical functionality will lead to a brittle and unsustainable architecture. To expand on this, consider that predictive scoring is often performed as part of some larger business process. Let's take a classic example of credit scoring. **Credit scoring** involves a base set of rules that have been defined manually and a set of models that are able to predict the likely outcome of the engagement with a given individual. Not only will the predictive models exist within a larger set of scoring mechanisms, such as rules, but all the scoring mechanisms will exist within the larger operational process of loan origination.

These operational systems can take many forms, from traditional ERP to more modern solutions, such as the ones based on Storm, which are dealing with web-scale operational process. The key is decoupling the iterative, analytical, and manual task of analytics from the low-latency, high-throughput, and highly available concerns of an operational solution. Within this context, PMML is extremely valuable.

In order to understand the model a little deeper, let's explore the content of PMML briefly. You can view the content of the model by opening the `random_forest.xml` file, which you generated as part of this recipe. What you will see is a model divided into many segments, and many "sub models". Each model is a tree structure of nodes, which are able to segment the feature space in a hierarchical manner until a leaf node is able to finally score the output for a given tree. Let's look at one example as shown in the following code snippet:

```
<Segment id="11">
    <True/>
```

```
    <TreeModel modelName="randomForest_Model"
functionName="classification" algorithmName="randomForest" splitCharac
teristic="binarySplit">
     <MiningSchema>
      <MiningField name="label" usageType="predicted"/>
      <MiningField name="v0" usageType="active"/>
      <MiningField name="v1" usageType="active"/>
      <MiningField name="v2" usageType="active"/>
      <MiningField name="v3" usageType="active"/>
      <MiningField name="v4" usageType="active"/>
      <MiningField name="v5" usageType="active"/>
      <MiningField name="v6" usageType="active"/>
      <MiningField name="v7" usageType="active"/>
      <MiningField name="v8" usageType="active"/>
      <MiningField name="v9" usageType="active"/>
     </MiningSchema>
     <Node id="1">
      <True/>
      <Node id="2">
       <SimplePredicate field="v0" operator="lessOrEqual"
value="1.025"/>
        <Node id="4">
        <SimplePredicate field="v3" operator="lessOrEqual"
value="0.15"/>
         <Node id="8" score="0">
          <SimplePredicate field="v5" operator="lessOrEqual"
value="0.76"/>
         </Node>
         <Node id="9">
          <SimplePredicate field="v5" operator="greaterThan"
value="0.76"/>
           <Node id="14" score="0">
            <SimplePredicate field="v0" operator="lessOrEqual"
value="0.305"/>
           </Node>
           <Node id="15" score="1">
            <SimplePredicate field="v0" operator="greaterThan"
value="0.305"/>
           </Node>
          </Node>
         </Node>
        <Node id="5">
         <SimplePredicate field="v3" operator="greaterThan"
value="0.15"/>
```

```xml
        <Node id="10">
        <SimplePredicate field="v5" operator="lessOrEqual"
value="0.19"/>
            <Node id="16" score="0">
            <SimplePredicate field="v4" operator="lessOrEqual"
value="0.48"/>
            </Node>
            <Node id="17">
            <SimplePredicate field="v4" operator="greaterThan"
value="0.48"/>
                <Node id="22">
                <SimplePredicate field="v4" operator="lessOrEqual"
value="1.04"/>
                    <Node id="26" score="0">
                    <SimplePredicate field="v1" operator="lessOrEqual"
value="-0.435"/>
                    </Node>
                    <Node id="27" score="1">
                    <SimplePredicate field="v1" operator="greaterThan"
value="-0.435"/>
                    </Node>
                </Node>
                <Node id="23" score="0">
                <SimplePredicate field="v4" operator="greaterThan"
value="1.04"/>
                </Node>
            </Node>
        </Node>
```

You will notice that the model specifies the algorithm and the type in terms of classification or regression. In this case, we have a Random Forest for classification. There is then a large set of nested `Node` elements. Each node has an ID and a predicate. The leaf nodes have a score. The predicate operators specify the operation to be performed by the scoring algorithm while it traverses the tree with a given set of input fields. Predicates can be simple Boolean operators (=, <, >, and so on) or compound predicates that combine many simple predicates using binary operators.

You may appreciate at this point, that this structure is extremely simple. The complexity is in the generation of the model. From this generated model, the scoring implementation should be comparatively simple.

Operational classification of transactional streams using Random Forest

Now that you have a built classification model, we need to implement an operational topology that leverages this model in order to perform classification as part of a larger operational data pipeline. I would like to draw a distinction between an operational data pipeline and an operational process. I will talk about operational process as an architecture concern that involves potentially many system layers. These may include ERP, CRM, core processing engine, and so on. An operational process is, therefore, positioned at the solution architecture level, and, as stated in the previous recipe, it typically won't include an analytics platform, such as R. A data pipeline is applicable at Trident's level of abstraction. Trident, in effect, allows you to define a streaming data pipeline. It abstracts away that state and planning in order to achieve this pipeline at scale and in parallel.

This recipe will therefore present operational scoring using a classification model as part of a Trident data pipeline that may exist within a larger operational process at the solution level.

The recipe illustrates this by implementing an order management topology. A stream of order data will flow into the order management topology, be unpacked, scored, and then finally enriched with distribution management information before being published. The ultimate destination being some kind of logistics management system will handle the logistics of delivering the order. The purpose is to show how scoring can be linked into a data flow that includes more than simply scoring.

Getting ready

To begin with, ensure that you have installed Kafka as per the instructions in the *Implementing a transactional topology* recipe within this chapter. Furthermore, ensure that Python is installed on your machine. This can be achieved using `apt-get`.

If you had any trouble building the Random Forest model, you can use the pre-built instance of the model from the code package associated with this chapter.

Please note that the testing scripts for the topology are contained in the supporting code for the chapter and are written in Python. The script that generates orders, generates JSON array order objects and places them on the appropriate Kafka topic.

How to do it...

1. Start by `creating` a Maven project called `rf-topology` and add the following dependencies:

```
<dependency>
    <groupId>com.github.quintona</groupId>
    <artifactId>trident-kafka-push</artifactId>
```

```xml
        <version>1.0-SNAPSHOT</version>
        <exclusions>
           <exclusion>
              <artifactId>storm</artifactId>
              <groupId>storm</groupId>
           </exclusion>
        </exclusions>
    </dependency>
    <dependency>
        <groupId>com.googlecode.json-simple</groupId>
        <artifactId>json-simple</artifactId>
        <version>1.1</version>
    </dependency>
    <dependency>
        <groupId>storm</groupId>
        <artifactId>storm-kafka</artifactId>
        <version>0.9.0-wip16b-scala292</version>
        <exclusions>
           <exclusion>
              <artifactId>storm</artifactId>
              <groupId>storm</groupId>
           </exclusion>
        </exclusions>
    </dependency>
    <dependency>
        <groupId>com.github.quintona</groupId>
        <artifactId>storm-pattern</artifactId>
        <version>0.0.3-SNAPSHOT</version>
        <exclusions>
           <exclusion>
              <artifactId>storm</artifactId>
              <groupId>storm</groupId>
           </exclusion>
        </exclusions>
    </dependency>
```

2. Next, create the `OrderManagementTopology` main class and implement a
    standard Storm main-method idiom. Next, you must create a function that will coerce
    the data into the correct format from the Kafka spout. This is done by converting the
    byte array into a string and parsing into a JSON array. The fields must also be parsed
    and typed correctly in the output tuple as follows:

```java
public static class CoerceInFunction extends BaseFunction {

    @Override
    public void execute(TridentTuple tuple, TridentCollector
colector) {
```

```
String text = new String(tuple.getBinary(0));
JSONArray array = (JSONArray) JSONValue.parse(text);
List<Object> values = new ArrayList<Object>(array.size());
String id = (String) array.get(array.size() - 1);
array.remove(array.size() - 1);
for(Object obj : array){
   values.add(Double.parseDouble((String)obj));
}
values.add(id);

if(array.size() > 0){
   collector.emit(new Values(values.toArray()));
}
}
}
```

3. As part of the flow of this topology, you will need to publish the content out to
    another Kafka topic. To achieve this, we will use a Trident module that leverages a
    partition persist. `KafkaStateUpdater` expects us to use the contents of a single
    configurable field to publish to the Kafka topic; therefore, our downstream tuple must
    be coerced into a single JSON array that can be published to downstream systems, as
    shown in the following lines of code:

```
public static class CoerceOutFunction extends BaseFunction {
   @Override
   public void execute(TridentTuple tuple, TridentCollector
                       collector) {
      JSONObject obj = new JSONObject();
      obj.put("order-id", tuple.getStringByField("order-id"));
      obj.put("dispatch-to", tuple.getStringByField(
                                        "dispatch-to"));
      collector.emit(new Values(obj.toJSONString()));
   }
}
```

4. Finally, you need to define the topology as follows:

```
topology.newStream("kafka",
            new TransactionalTridentKafkaSpout(spoutConfig))
               .each(new Fields("bytes"), new
                     CoerceInFunction(),new Fields(allFields))
               .each(new Fields(valueNames), new
                     ClassifierFunction("/usr/local/random_forest
                     .xml"), new Fields("prediction"))
               .each(new Fields("prediction"),
                     new Debug("Prediction"))
```

```
                      .each(new Fields("prediction"),
                          new EnrichFunction(), new Fields(
                          "dispatch-to"))
                      .each(new Fields("order-id", "dispatch-to"),
                          new CoerceOutFunction(),new
                          Fields("message"))
                      .partitionPersist(KafkaState.transactional(
                          "order-output", new KafkaState.Options()),
                          new Fields("message"), new
                          KafkaStateUpdater("message"),
                          new Fields("message"));
```

The following diagram clarifies the data pipeline of this topology:

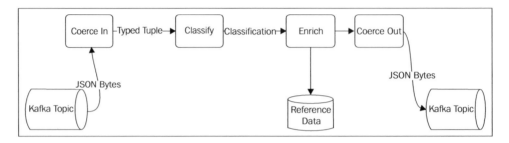

Complete your topology by providing the Kafka configuration as per the *Implementing a transactional topology* recipe using the `orders` topic. Then run your topology in the local mode.

You can test it using the `sendOrders.py` Python script as described here:

python sendOrders.py 1000 10

The script takes two arguments, the number of orders to generate and the number of features to add to each order. You can use any value for the first argument, but the topology expects exactly 10 features as it currently stands. If you want to adjust the number of features, you will need to change your topology.

How it works...

The focus here is on the `classifier` function. The function itself is quite simple; it takes a string during construction and uses it to initialize a classifier at preparation time. When a tuple is received within the function, it simply delegates to the classifier as follows:

```
public void execute(TridentTuple tuple, TridentCollector collector) {
    String label = classifier.classifyTuple(tuple);
```

```
        collector.emit(new Values(label));
    }
```

The `classifier` function builds an underlying model by parsing the XML node structure and building an in-memory **Directed Acyclic Graph** (**DAG**) of the node and predicate hierarchy. With a complete graph, all that is required at classification/scoring time is to walk the graph, apply each predicate, and receive a final output value. In the case of a Random Forest, the outputs must be further ranked, because it is a forest of trees and executed as follows:

```
public String classifyTuple(TridentTuple values) throws
PatternException {
        Boolean[] pred_eval = context.evalPredicates(schema, values);
        String label = null;
        Integer winning_vote = 0;
        votes.clear();
        // tally the vote for each tree in the forest

        for (Model model : segments) {
            label = ((TreeModel) model).tree.traverse(pred_eval);

            if (!votes.containsKey(label))
                winning_vote = 1;
            else
                winning_vote = votes.get(label) + 1;

            votes.put(label, winning_vote);
        }
        // determine the winning label
        for (String key : votes.keySet()) {
            if (votes.get(key) > winning_vote) {
                label = key;
                winning_vote = votes.get(key);
            }
        }

        return label;
    }
```

Another piece of topology worth the explanation is the Kafka Push partition persist, and is executed as follows:

```
.partitionPersist(KafkaState.transactional("order-output",
            new KafkaState.Options()), new Fields("message"),
            new KafkaStateUpdater("message"), new Fields("message"));
```

A partition persist operation is typically reserved for database-like backers, not message queues. In this case, it is important to publish using a partition persist in order to support the transactional semantics. One can't simply publish from within a Trident function if they intend to support transactional semantics. `KafkaState` ensures that messages are only published to Kafka once the transaction commits as described here:

```
public void beginCommit(Long txid) {
        if(messages.size() > 0)
            throw new RuntimeException("Kafka State is invalid, the
previous transaction didn't flush");
    }

    public void enqueue(String message){
        if(transactional)
            messages.add(message);
        else
            sendMessage(message);
    }

    private void sendMessage(String message){
        ProducerData<String, String> data = new ProducerData<String,
                                       String>(topic, message);
        producer.send(data);
    }

    @Override
    public void commit(Long txid) {
        String message = messages.poll();
        while(message != null){
            sendMessage(message);
            message = messages.poll();
        }
    }
```

 For more details of the Kafka Push partition persist, please review the code in KafkaState at `https://github.com/quintona/trident-kafka-push/blob/master/src/main/java/com/github/quintona/KafkaState.java`.

There's more...

You may ask yourself how the model is able to make sense of randomly generated data? The answer is that the model can't make sense of randomly generated data. There has to be an inherent relationship/concept/abstraction in the data that the model can find in order for the model to predict any more accurately than a coin toss. It is therefore important to create some relationship within the numbers that are generated from the testing script. The provided script is, therefore, an interesting starting point for learning purposes. The script works by defining a set of distributions that are segmented according to a set of probabilities. For each row, a random value is used to choose the appropriate segment. Each segment in turn generates a value based on a Gaussian distribution with set mean and standard deviation values per segment. This approach leaves something tangible for the model to find and predict against, while still having enough variability to be interesting. The code snippet is described as follows:

```
CUSTOMER_SEGMENTS = (
    [0.2, ["0", random.gauss, 0.25, 0.75, "%0.2f"]],
    [0.8, ["0", random.gauss, 1.5, 0.25, "%0.2f"]],
    [0.9, ["1", random.gauss, 0.6, 0.2, "%0.2f"]],
    [1.0, ["1", random.gauss, 0.75, 0.2, "%0.2f"]]
)

def gen_row (segments, num_col):
    coin_flip = random.random()

    for prob, rand_var in segments:
        if coin_flip <= prob:
            (label, dist, mean, sigma, format) = rand_var
            order_id = str(uuid.uuid1()).split("-")[0]
            return map(lambda x: format % dist(mean, sigma), range(
            0, num_col)) + [order_id]
```

 Note that this script is tested with Python 2.7, and some changes may be required if you use Python 3 and above.

Creating an association rules model in R

At present, the Storm Pattern Project supports the following set of models:

- Random Forest
- Linear Regression
- Hierarchical Clustering and K-means clustering
- Logistic Regression

While these models cover an extremely wide range of use cases, there are many more algorithms that aren't represented. It is obviously desirable, for various reasons, to have a native implementation of the model within Storm, and the community is working towards supporting a wider base; however, it must be noted that it is unlikely that the Storm community will build out machine learning support at the same speed as the R community, given the sheer size difference of focus from that community. As a result, when there is an algorithm that you need to use that isn't support by Storm-Pattern, making use of R becomes a viable option (or you could build it and contribute it back to the community).

I realize that I elaborated somewhat in the previous recipe as to analytical systems not polluting the operational architecture; this approach appears to contradict this, but in fact it doesn't. This deserves some clarification. R is, in many ways, like a Unix system; it is highly modular. As a result, you can choose to use as much or as little as you like from the community of packages and capabilities. If you think about Ubuntu, you can run it without any X-Windows system, purely at the command line, which makes it highly versatile in many environments. R shares this quality. Mixing a full R environment into an operational system may not be the correct approach; however, allowing Storm Bolts to manage the `vanilla` and `slave` R instances across a Storm cluster allows R to simply augment the Storm functionality rather than represent another architecturally significant component or layer from a functional perspective.

A popular use case for machine learning is a recommendation engine. *People who choose these options, often chose this option, so you should too.* There are various ways to achieve this, and a popular approach is to use association rules. R has an excellent implementation of association rules in the `arules` package. This recipe seeks to demonstrate how to build a set of association rules that we will use later to build a recommendation engine in Storm using the model we have created.

Getting ready

In order to implement this recipe, you need to have the `arules` package installed. Start by installing it using the following command from within RStudio:

```
install.packages("arules")
```

How to do it...

1. For this example, we are going to use a dataset that is packaged with R. Load the `arules` package and load the `Groceries` dataset:

   ```
   library("arules")
   data("Groceries")
   ```

2. We now need to explore the data and get an idea of what we are dealing with. Execute the `summary(Groceries)` command, and you should receive an output similar to the following screenshot:

```
transactions as itemMatrix in sparse format with
 9835 rows (elements/itemsets/transactions) and
 169 columns (items) and a density of 0.02609146

most frequent items:
      whole milk other vegetables      rolls/buns
            2513                1903          1809
      soda              yogurt       (Other)
            1715                1372          34055

element (itemset/transaction) length distribution:
sizes
   1    2    3    4    5    6    7    8    9   10   11
2159 1643 1299 1005  855  645  545  438  350  246  182

  12   13   14   15   16   17   18   19   20   21   22   23   24   26
 117   78   77   55   46   29   14   14    9   11    4    6    1    1

  27   28   29   32
   1    1    3    1

  Min. 1st Qu.  Median    Mean 3rd Qu.    Max.
 1.000   2.000   3.000   4.409   6.000  32.000

includes extended item information - examples:
      labels   level2              level1
1 frankfurter sausage meet and sausage
2     sausage sausage meet and sausage
3  liver loaf sausage meet and sausage
```

The data essentially consists of tab-separated lists of items, where each row represents a list of items that were purchased together. It is easy to imagine how such a dataset could be constructed in something like a grocery store.

3. We can now build some rules as follows:

```
rules <- apriori(Groceries, parameter = list(supp = 0.001, conf = 0.8))

print(rules)

print(summary(rules))
```

4. It is often useful to see the rules with the highest lift for validation purposes execute; this is shown in the following command:

```
rules_high_lift <- head(sort(rules, by="lift"), 4)

inspect(rules_high_lift)
```

5. The output should look similar to the following image:

```
lhs                                rhs                   support confidence       lift
1 {liquor,
   red/blush wine}        => {bottled beer}    0.001931876  0.9047619 11.235269
2 {citrus fruit,
   other vegetables,
   soda,
   fruit/vegetable juice} => {root vegetables} 0.001016777  0.9090909  8.340400
3 {tropical fruit,
   other vegetables,
   whole milk,
   yogurt,
   oil}                  => {root vegetables} 0.001016777  0.9090909  8.340400
4 {citrus fruit,
   grapes,
   fruit/vegetable juice} => {tropical fruit}  0.001118454  0.8461538  8.063879
```

6. What this tells us is that when `liquor` and `red` are selected together, the customer will likely choose `beer`, so you should recommend that to him to increase the chances of that sale. Now that we have a model, we just need to save it as follows:

```
saveXML(pmml(rules), file=paste(dat_folder, "groc.arules.xml",
sep="/"))
```

How it works...

Association rules are based on two concepts:

▶ The support of an item set is the proportion of the overall transactions that contain the particular item set

▶ The confidence is probably that a set of items on the LHS will result in the given item on the RHS of the rule

The algorithm, in this case being Apriori, uses these concepts to derive and rank the rules it finds in the transactional data. The `lift` value ranks the results of the rule against a random choice model. The `lift` measure gives us confidence that the prediction will give us much better results than simply randomly choosing another product to recommend.

Creating a recommendation engine

A recommendation engine makes intelligent guesses as to what a customer may want to buy based on previous lists of products, which has been made famous by leaders such as Amazon. These lists may be from a current selection within the context of the current session. The list of products may be from previous purchases by the particular customer, and it may even simply be the products that the customer has viewed within a given session. Whichever approach you choose, the training data and scoring data during operational phases must follow the same principles.

In this recipe, we will use the association rules model from the previous recipe to create a recommendation engine. The concept behind the engine is that lists are supplied as asynchronous inputs and recommendations are forwarded as asynchronous outputs where applicable.

 There are product combinations that aren't strongly supported by the model; in these cases, no recommendation is emitted. If you need a recommendation for every single input, you could choose to emit a random recommendation when there is no strongly supported recommendation, or you could choose to improve your model through better and generally larger training datasets.

How to do it...

1. Start by creating a Maven project called `arules-topology` and add the following dependencies:

```
<dependency>
        <groupId>com.github.quintona</groupId>
        <artifactId>trident-kafka-push</artifactId>
        <version>1.0-SNAPSHOT</version>
</dependency>
<dependency>
        <groupId>storm</groupId>
        <artifactId>storm-kafka</artifactId>
        <version>0.9.0-wip16b-scala292</version>
</dependency>
<dependency>
        <groupId>com.github.quintona</groupId>
        <artifactId>storm-r</artifactId>
        <version>0.0.1-SNAPSHOT</version>
</dependency>
```

2. Next, create a main topology class called `RecommendationTopology` using the idiomatic Storm main method. For this recipe, we will be receiving the product list as a JSON array on a Kafka topic. We will therefore need to coerce the byte array input into a tuple containing two separate values, one being the transaction ID and the other being the list of products, as shown in the following lines of code:

```
public static class CoerceInFunction extends BaseFunction {

        @Override
        public void execute(TridentTuple tuple, TridentCollector
                                collector) {
            String text = new String(tuple.getBinary(0));
            JSONArray array = (JSONArray) JSONValue.parse(text);
```

```
            List<String> values = new ArrayList<String>(array.
                                size()-1);
            String id = (String) array.get(0);
            array.remove(0);
            for(Object obj : array){
               values.add((String)obj);
            }
            if(array.size() > 0){
               collector.emit(new Values(id, values));
            }
         }
      }
   }
```

3. We will also need to publish the output message using the Kafka partition persist. The recommendation and transaction ID need to be coerced into a single value consisting of a JSON array as follows:

```
public static class CoerceOutFunction extends BaseFunction {
      @Override
      public void execute(TridentTuple tuple, TridentCollector
                            collector) {
         JSONObject obj = new JSONObject();
         obj.put("transaction-id", tuple
               .getStringByField("transaction-id"));
         obj.put("recommendation", tuple.getStringByField(
               "recommendation"));
         collector.emit(new Values(obj.toJSONString()));
      }
}
```

4. We then need to define the topology as described here:

```
topology.newStream("kafka",
             new TransactionalTridentKafkaSpout(spoutConfig))
                .each(new Fields("bytes"), new
                     CoerceInFunction(),new Fields(
                     "transaction-id","current-list"))
                .each(new Fields("current-list"), new
                     ListRFunction(Arrays.asList(new String[] {
                     "arules" }), "recommend")
                     .withNamedInitCode("recommend"),
                     new Fields("recommendation"))
                .each(new Fields("transaction-id",
                     "recommendation"),
                     new CoerceOutFunction(),
                     new Fields("message"))
                .partitionPersist(KafkaState
                     .transactional("recommendation-output",
```

```
                        new KafkaState.Options()),
                        new Fields("message"),
                        new KafkaStateUpdater("message"),
                        new Fields());
```

5. The Storm-R project's standard function supports only a known input array size. This works for most use cases; however, for the association case, the input size will vary for each tuple. It is therefore necessary to override the `execute` function to cater for this particular case as shown here:

```
public static class ListRFunction extends RFunction {

        public ListRFunction(List<String> libraries, String
                               functionName) {
           super(libraries, functionName);
        }

        @Override
        public void execute(TridentTuple tuple, TridentCollector
                               collector) {
           List<String> items = (List<String>) tuple.get(0);
           JSONArray functionInput = new JSONArray();
           functionInput.addAll(items);
           JSONArray result = performFunction(functionInput);
           if(result != null)
              collector.emit(coerceResponce(result));
        }

    }
```

6. These elements are all that is required to create the recommendation engine. You can now start your topology in local mode from Eclipse. In order to test it, a test script is provided with the chapter code bundle named `sendSelection.py`. This takes a single parameter, which is the number of transactions, to publish onto the queue as follows:

```
python sendSelection.py 1000
```

7. You can view the output recommendations by issuing the following command from the Kafka command line:

```
bin/kafka-console-consumer.sh --zookeeper localhost:2181 --topic
recommendation-output --from-beginning
```

How it works...

At the fundamental level, Storm-R works in a very similar way to the multilang approach that we investigated in detail in *Chapter 5, Polyglot Topology*. For each instance of the function, it creates an R process that it interacts with via Studio. However, Storm-R cuts much of the complexity and overhead out because it doesn't make use of a generalized protocol; it is specific to R. This makes it much faster and simpler.

The key assumption behind Storm-R is that a single R function will be called from the Storm function and will pass a vector as input. The R function will return a vector as output. This assumption nicely aligns the function interface with the concept of a tuple. The Storm-R module further simplifies the R implementation by auto-generating some code to take care of the marshaling and unmarshaling of the vector across the interface.

As with a standard Trident function, any lengthy functions should execute during the preparation phase of the Storm function. The Storm-R function expects to be initialized with a function name and a list of R libraries to load during the preparation phase. It can also take an R script that should be executed during the preparation phase.

The R function that is to be called needs to be available within the R session. This means that the R function needs to be supplied in a prebuilt package, or it can be defined in the initialization script. In this recipe, we are using a function that is defined in the initialization script, but specifically we are using a prepackaged initialization script that ships with Storm-R.

Let's unpack the R function definition within the topology with the following code snippet:

```
.each(new Fields("current-list"), new ListRFunction(Arrays.asList(new
     String[] { "arules" }), "recommend")
     .withNamedInitCode("recommend"), new Fields("recommendation"))
```

Firstly, the constructor receives a list of libraries to load into R; in this case, just the `arules` package. The constructor also receives a function name called `recommend`. This is the R function that will receive a vector input and must return a vector output. Secondly, the `withNamedInitCode` method is called and the name `recommend` is supplied. What this function does is look up a script on the classpath by appending `.R` to the name supplied. Therefore, in this case, a script named `/recommend.R` is present at the root of the classpath. This means that you can supply any script there, but in this case, we will use the one that Storm-R brings to the classpath. There is also an overloaded method that allows you to supply the script's contents as a string.

Let's take a look at the contents of the `recommend` script as shown here:

```
data("Groceries")

rules <- apriori(Groceries, parameter = list(supp = 0.001, conf = 0.8)

recommend <- function(list){
```

```
    rules.found <- subset(rules, subset = lhs %ain% list & lift > 1.3)
    as(rhs(rules.found), "list")
}
```

You will notice some things from the previous recipe. Essentially, this script is loading the dataset and building the rules from it. It is then defining a function called `recommend` that takes a vector as input and uses it to search the rules for any found matches where the lift is greater than 1.3 and the LHS is the supplied input list. It then converts the RHS of the found rules into a vector and returns.

 There are three ways to match using the subset function: `Any`, `All`, or `Partial`. This example uses `All` (`%ain%`); however, you could choose a less script-matching criteria such as `Any` (`%in%`) or `Partial` (`%pin%`).

The net effect is that at the time of Trident function preparation, the library will be loaded, and this function will be defined, making it available for all subsequent calls in the session. All subsequent calls will originate from the `execute` method and contain the values from tuple.

In this recipe, we overrode the `execute` method of `RFunction`. The reason, as stated, is that the standard implementation expects a fixed set of values in the tuple. This becomes more apparent when you compare the implementations. The `execute` method from `RFunction` consists of the following code:

```
JSONArray functionInput = coerceTuple(tuple);
    JSONArray result = performFunction(functionInput);
    if(result != null)
        collector.emit(coerceResponce(result));
```

Whereas the overridden version consists of the following code:

```
List<String> items = (List<String>) tuple.get(0);
        JSONArray functionInput = new JSONArray();
        functionInput.addAll(items);
        JSONArray result = performFunction(functionInput);
        if(result != null)
            collector.emit(coerceResponce(result));
```

As you can see, the difference is subtle but important. The first instance uses the values of the tuple as the input to the R function. The second instance uses the content of one of the values of the tuple, which is an array itself. In this way, we can support any length of products.

There's more...

The test script is built with a complete list of all possible products. For each message it publishes, it simply creates a random number of products, between 2 and 5, and populates them randomly from the total population of products:

```
products = ["".....""]
def get_values():
    vals = []
    for i in range(0,random.randint(2,5)):
        rn = random.randint(0,len(products)-1)
        candidate = products[rn]
        while vals.count(candidate) == 1:
            rn = random.randint(0,len(products)-1)
            candidate = products[rn]
        vals.append(candidate)
    return vals

def gen_row():
    row = get_values()
    row.insert(0,str(uuid.uuid1()).split("-")[0])
    return row
```

Real-time online machine learning

The process of performing predictive analytics is largely iterative and interactive in nature; however, in all the previous examples, there is a definite distinction between the learning phase and the scoring phase within the life of the model. In the case of online learning algorithms, this line gets blurred. An online learning algorithm learns continuously through streams of updated training data. Algorithms are therefore said to be either batch-based or online. Note that, in either case, the algorithm can be real-time; however, in the batch-based model, a model is built in some offline batch process and is deployed into Storm for the purposes of real-time scoring. In the online case, the algorithm both learns and scores as it sees new data and is also deployed into Storm as the real-time processing engine.

This recipe implements an online **Regression Perceptron**. What this name simply means is that the algorithm learns in an online manner and the predictions are non-discreet. The perceptron therefore predicts continuous values, not discreet classifications.

 For more information on classification and regression, please read the Wikipedia pages on both topics at http://en.wikipedia.org/wiki/Statistical_classification and http://en.wikipedia.org/wiki/Regression_analysis.

How to do it...

1. Create a new Storm topology Maven project called `online-ml-topology` with the following dependencies:

```
<dependency>
          <groupId>com.github.pmerienne</groupId>
          <artifactId>trident-ml</artifactId>
          <version>0.0.3-SNAPSHOT</version>
</dependency>
<dependency>
          <groupId>com.github.quintona</groupId>
          <artifactId>trident-kafka-push</artifactId>
          <version>1.0-SNAPSHOT</version>
</dependency>
```

2. Using Eclipse, create the `OnlineTopology` main class, and implement the idiomatic Storm main method. For this topology, we will have two input streams, one for the training data and one for the data to be scored. In order to deal with the training data, we need to coerce the input JSON message into doubles as follows:

```
public static class CoerceInSample extends BaseFunction {
     @Override
     public void execute(TridentTuple tuple, TridentCollector
                          collector) {
          String text = new String(tuple.getBinary(0));
          JSONArray array = (JSONArray) JSONValue.parse(text);
          Double[] values = new Double[array.size()];
          for(int i = 0; i < array.size(); i++){
             values[i] = ((Number)array.get(i)).doubleValue();
          }
          if(array.size() > 0){
            collector.emit(new Values(values));
          }
     }
}
```

3. The scoring input stream is very similar; however, it also contains a transaction ID, which we need to deal with, and type validity, which is important, as shown here:

```
public static class CoerceInTransaction extends BaseFunction {
     @Override
     public void execute(TridentTuple tuple, TridentCollector
                          collector) {
          String text = new String(tuple.getBinary(0));
          JSONArray array = (JSONArray) JSONValue.parse(text);
          String id = (String)array.remove(array.size() - 1);
```

```
            List<Object> values = new ArrayList<Object>(
                                array.size());
            for(int i = 0; i < array.size(); i++){
                values.add(((Number)array.get(i)).doubleValue());
            }
            values.add(id);
            if(array.size() > 0){
                collector.emit(new Values(values.toArray()));
            }
        }
    }
}
```

4. As with previous recipes, you will need to coerce the output into a single JSON message so that it can be published to Kafka as follows:

```
public static class CoerceOutFunction extends BaseFunction {
        @Override
        public void execute(TridentTuple tuple, TridentCollector
                            collector) {
            JSONObject obj = new JSONObject();
            obj.put("transaction-id", tuple
                    .getStringByField("transaction-id"));
            obj.put("prediction", tuple.getDoubleByField(
                    "prediction"));
            collector.emit(new Values(obj.toJSONString()));
        }
    }
}
```

5. Finally, you will need to define the spouts and topology, as described in the following code snippet:

```
TridentState perceptronModel = topology.newStream("labeleddata",
        new TransactionalTridentKafkaSpout(trainingSpoutConfig))
                .each(new Fields("bytes"), new CoerceInSample(),
                    new Fields("f1","f2","f3","f4","label"))
                .each(new Fields("label", "f1","f2","f3","f4"),
                    new InstanceCreator<Double>(),
                    new Fields("instance"))
                .partitionPersist(new MemoryMapState.Factory(),
                    new Fields("instance"),
                    new RegressionUpdater("perceptron",
                    new PerceptronRegressor()));

        topology.newStream("transactions",
            new TransactionalTridentKafkaSpout(
                                        scoringSpoutConfig))
```

```
.each(new Fields("bytes"),
        new CoerceInTransaction(), new Fields(
        "f1","f2","f3","f4","transaction-id"))
.each(new Fields("f1","f2","f3","f4"),
        new InstanceCreator<Double>(false),
        new Fields("instance"))
.stateQuery(perceptronModel,
        new Fields("instance"),
        new RegressionQuery("perceptron"),
        new Fields("prediction"))
.each(new Fields("transaction-id", "prediction"),
        new CoerceOutFunction(),
        new Fields("message"))
.partitionPersist(KafkaState
        .transactional("prediction-output",
        new KafkaState.Options()),
        new Fields("message"),
        new KafkaStateUpdater("message"),
        new Fields());
```

6. At this point you can run the topology in local mode; in order to test it, you will need to run the supplied scripts as follows:

   python sendLabeledData.py 1000

   python sendTransactions.py 1000

7. Both scripts take the number of records as input arguments. You can view the scored transactional data by using the following command:

   bin/kafka-console-consumer.sh --zookeeper localhost:2181 --topic prediction-output --from-beginning

How it works...

This approach works by maintaining some shared state, specifically the weights within the perceptron. One stream of data updates these weights, and the second stream reads them as part of the scoring process.

Let's unpack how the model is trained in the online mode, as shown in the following lines of code:

```
TridentState perceptronModel = topology.newStream("labeleddata",
            new TransactionalTridentKafkaSpout(trainingSpoutConfig))
        .each(new Fields("bytes"), new CoerceInSample(),
            new Fields("f1","f2","f3","f4","label"))
        .each(new Fields("label", "f1","f2","f3","f4"),
            new InstanceCreator<Double>(),
            new Fields("instance"))
```

```
                .partitionPersist(new MemoryMapState.Factory(),
                        new Fields("instance"),
                        new RegressionUpdater("perceptron",
                        new PerceptronRegressor())));
```

Firstly, the data is coerced into the correct format and converted into an instance. Take note that the order of the fields differs between the spout and the label instance creator. The instance creator expects the label in the first value, but the input message contains the label in the last field. This is dealt with easily, because Trident effectively projects the value. The instance is then used to update the regression model as part of a partition persist of state where the state is backed into a memory map.

 The state could easily have been backed by Memcached or Cassandra or any other persistence mechanism that you choose as is the case with any other state in Trident.

The regression model itself is updated and then saved as part of the update functionality within the partition persist step as shown here:

```
Instance<Double> instance;
for (TridentTuple tuple : tuples) {
    instance = (Instance<Double>) tuple.get(0);
    regressor.update(instance.label, instance.features);
}
state.multiPut(KeysUtil.toKeys(this.classifierName),
            Arrays.asList(regressor));
```

The underlying `PerceptronRegressor` simply updates its weights based on the supplied labeled data and its error function.

With an updated model in memory, the model can simply be used for scoring. A second stream deals with this as follows:

```
TransactionalTridentKafkaSpout(scoringSpoutConfig))
            .each(new Fields("bytes"), new CoerceInTransaction(),
                new Fields("f1","f2","f3","f4","transaction-id"))
            .each(new Fields("f1","f2","f3","f4"),
                new InstanceCreator<Double>(false),
                new Fields("instance"))
            .stateQuery(perceptronModel, new Fields("instance"),
                new RegressionQuery("perceptron"),
                new Fields("prediction"))
            .each(new Fields("transaction-id", "prediction"),
                new CoerceOutFunction(),new Fields("message"))
            .partitionPersist(KafkaState.transactional(
                "prediction-output", new KafkaState.Options()),
                new Fields("message"),
                new KafkaStateUpdater("message"), new Fields());
```

In this case, the input is also coerced into an instance, but this time the instance is used to query the state. The query will retrieve the regression model and then use it to predict new values, as shown in the following code snippet:

```
Double label;
  Instance<Double> instance;
  for (TridentTuple tuple : tuples) {
      instance = (Instance<Double>) tuple.get(0);
      label = regressor.predict(instance.features);
      labels.add(label);
  }
```

In this way, the model is learning in an online mode as it "sees" new data. This updated view is made available to the scoring stream because of the inherent power in the state management model of Trident.

8
Continuous Delivery

In this chapter we will cover:

- ► Setting up a CI server
- ► Setting up system environments
- ► Defining a delivery pipeline
- ► Implementing automated acceptance testing

Introduction

Continuous Delivery is a term coined by *Martin Fowler* in his book by the same name. I won't try to duplicate his work here, but as an extremely brief introduction, Continuous Delivery is a natural extension of Continuous Integration. The base concept behind Continuous Delivery is that IT risks are best dealt with by failing small and failing often. The longer it takes you to integrate a system, the larger the risk will be. So rather integrate often; this way you experience the "pain" of integration in small bite-size chunks. Off the back of this concept, Continuous Integration was born, enabled with many excellent tool suites. Continuous Delivery extends the concept by recognizing that the process of operational deployment is also extremely risky and reaches a point where many IT projects fail. The longer you take to perform a deployment, the greater the risk. So rather experience the "pain" of deployment as early as possible in small bite size chunks. As with Continuous Integration, a key focus then becomes speed and automation. If we are going to integrate often, it needs to involve as little effort as possible and be regressive in nature, meaning that we don't redo the same tasks repetitively.

The other key recognition from Continuous Delivery is that we as IT professionals have only delivered once we have delivered something into a production environment and it is adding value to the business and users it serves. Until that point, we only represent a cost.

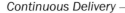

With these thoughts in mind, we will explore how to implement Continuous Delivery on Storm-based systems. In this chapter, we will set up Jenkins as our Continuous Integration server; that along with some configuration, will also act as a Continuous Delivery server. We will then set up our environment tooling, establish a reliable build, deploy, and accept test cycle.

In the next chapter, we will learn how to deploy Storm into the AWS cloud, at which point we will complete the delivery process.

Setting up a CI server

Jenkins is one of the most widely used open CI servers (http://jenkins-ci.org/). Jenkins is a fork of the Hudson CI, which occurred in 2010 as a result of disputes between the community and Oracle over project control issues. Since the project split, there has been a growing support base for Jenkins. Evaluating tool choices is often difficult, and you must obviously evaluate various options before choosing the correct tool for your situation. Jenkins is chosen here because it is one of the leading open source options and is known to be widely used and supported.

Getting ready

We will install Jenkins into a Vagrant-based VirtualBox. This will allow you to build and test your environment in a portable way, and push it to various cloud providers later.

How to do it...

1. Create a new project folder and initialize the Vagrant configuration file:

   ```
   mkdir vagrant-jenkins
   cd vagrant-jenkins
   vagrant init
   ```

2. This will generate a Vagrant file for you. You can review the comments in the file, then update the file to reflect the following properties, which will create a 64-bit Ubuntu precise instance with a Puppet-based provisioning script:

   ```
   Vagrant.configure("2") do |config|
     config.vm.box = "precise64"
     config.vm.box_url = "http://files.vagrantup.com/precise64.box"
     config.vm.network :private_network, ip: "192.168.33.11"
     config.vm.synced_folder "./data", "/vagrant_data"
     config.vm.provider :virtualbox do |vb|
       vb.customize ["modifyvm", :id, "--memory", "1024"]
     end
     config.vm.provision :puppet
   end
   ```

You may need to adjust your network settings depending on your situation. Please review the Vagrant documentation at `http://docs.vagrantup.com/v2/networking/index.html` for further details.

3. You must then create the Jenkins Puppet provisioning script. To do this, create two folders within the project called `manifests` and `data`. Within `manifests`, add a file called `default.pp` that adds the Jenkins package repository to the list of sources and installs Jenkins:

```
$key_url = "http://pkg.jenkins-ci.org/debian/jenkins-ci.org.key"
    $repo_url = "deb http://pkg.jenkins-ci.org/debian binary/"
    $apt_sources = "/etc/apt/sources.list"

    exec { "install jenkins key":
        command     => "wget -q -O - ${key_url} | apt-key
                       add -; echo '${repo_url}' >> ${apt_sources}",
        onlyif      => "grep -Fvxq '${repo_url}'
                       ${apt_sources}",
        path        => ["/bin", "/usr/bin"],
    }

    exec { "jenkins-apt-update":
        command => "/usr/bin/aptitude -y update",
        require => Exec["install jenkins key"],
    }

    package { "jenkins":
        ensure      => present,
        provider    => "aptitude",
        require     => Exec["jenkins-apt-update"],
    }

    service { "jenkins":
        enable      => true,
        ensure      => running,
        hasrestart  => true,
        hasstatus   => true,
        require     => Package["jenkins"],
    }
```

4. You can now bring up the Jenkins instance:

```
vagrant up
```

How it works...

This recipe is surprisingly simple. We have a base Vagrant configuration that brings up a single node, based on a `precise64` base box. Within this box, we simply install Jenkins using the Ubuntu packages. Because the packages aren't in the default universe, we have to add them and the associated keys first:

```
exec { "install jenkins key":
        command     => "wget -q -O - ${key_url} | apt-key add -;
                        echo '${repo_url}' >> ${apt_sources}",
        onlyif      => "grep -Fvxq '${repo_url}' ${apt_sources}",
        path        => ["/bin", "/usr/bin"],
    }
```

The package is then installed, and the service is brought up using the standard package and service types.

Setting up system environments

Automating all your environments is critical, but the first step in this process is to understand how to establish a stable environment from scratch for your particular solution. Once this process has been validated, it is then easy to automate and add into the pipeline. In this recipe, we will manually establish a complete environment for Jenkins.

Getting ready

We will use the Random Forest topology from *Chapter 7, Real-time Machine Learning*, as the project that will be managed by our Jenkins CI. In order to build and deploy this project, there are a number of things that must be installed into our CI:

- Oracle JDK
- SBT
- Apache Kafka
- Start by downloading the Oracle JDK from `http://www.oracle.com/technetwork/java/javase/downloads/index.html` and placing it in the `data` folder.

How to do it...

1. Connect to your Ubuntu instance using Vagrant SSH. Then, issue the following commands to clear the existing `openjdk`, and install the Oracle JDK:

   ```
   sudo apt-get purge openjdk-\*
   sudo mkdir -p /usr/local/java
   ```

```
sudo cp -r /vagrant_data/jdk-7u21-linux-x64.gz /usr/local/java
cd /usr/local/java
sudo tar xvzf jdk-7u21-linux-x64.gz
```

2. You must now edit `/etc/profile` and add the following code to it:

```
JAVA_HOME=/usr/local/java/jdk1.7.0_21
PATH=$PATH:$HOME/bin:$JAVA_HOME/bin
JRE_HOME=/usr/local/java/jdk1.7.0_21/jre
PATH=$PATH:$HOME/bin:$JRE_HOME/bin
export JAVA_HOME
export JRE_HOME
export PATH
```

3. You now need to update all the Java references across the system:

```
sudo update-alternatives --install "/usr/bin/java" "java" "/usr/
local/java/jdk1.7.0_21/jre/bin/java" 1
```

```
sudo update-alternatives --install "/usr/bin/javac" "javac" "/usr/
local/java/jdk1.7.0_21/bin/javac" 1
```

```
sudo update-alternatives --set java /usr/local/java/jdk1.7.0_21/
jre/bin/java
```

```
sudo update-alternatives --set javac /usr/local/java/jdk1.7.0_21/
bin/javac
```

```
. /etc/profile
```

4. In order to install Kafka, start by downloading the source packages from `https://www.apache.org/dyn/closer.cgi/incubator/kafka/kafka-0.7.2-incubating/kafka-0.7.2-incubating-src.tgz`. Once the download is complete, install **Scala Build Tool** (**SBT**), and then unpack and build the Kafka server:

```
cd ~
```

```
wget http://mirror.ventraip.net.au/apache/incubator/kafka/kafka-
0.7.2-incubating/kafka-0.7.2-incubating-src.tgz
```

```
wget http://apt.typesafe.com/repo-deb-build-0002.deb
```

```
sudo dpkg -i repo-deb-build-0002.deb
```

```
sudo apt-get update
```

```
sudo apt-get install sbt
```

```
tar xzf kafka-0.7.2-incudbating-src.tgz
```

```
cd kafka-0.7.2-incubating-src
```

```
./sbt update
```

```
./sbt package
```

5. Finally, you need to check whether your build is working on the CI server before attempting the build in the Jenkins software:

```
cd ~
wget https://raw.github.com/technomancy/leiningen/stable/bin/lein
sudo mv lein /usr/bin
sudo chmod +x /usr/bin/lein
git clone git://github.com/nathanmarz/storm-contrib.git
git clone https://bitbucket.org/qanderson/rf-topology.git
cd storm-contrib/storm-kafka
lein javac
lein install
cd ../rf-topology
mvn clean package
```

 You can replace the previous `clone` command with a URL to your repository.

How it works...

This is a really simple process, and a familiar one to you. The key here is that you validate your build and release process within your CI, which is different from your local development environment.

You will notice that I have checked out the `storm-contrib` module in order to build `storm-kafka`. This is because this module isn't deployed into any binary repository at present. I would suggest that you clone and deploy your own version of the `contrib` modules if binary version control is important to you or your organization.

Defining a delivery pipeline

The delivery pipeline not only ensures what is released is stable and controlled, but also enables this to be done rapidly. A pipeline can potentially enable every source commit to be a release candidate. The pipeline needs to be built out in distinct steps, each removing different kinds of risks from the delivery process. The following is an example of a build pipeline:

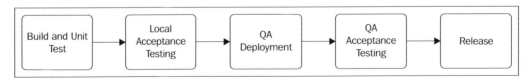

You will need to define a pipeline that is appropriate to your technology and organizational process.

The first step is the traditional CI step. This ensures that the code base is built and is unit tested. It is important to keep the build and unit test process to a very short time, thus allowing developers to receive rapid feedback on their changes. It is also necessary to perform a more complete test of the code base in a deployed or semi-deployed form. This can be divided into integration tests and acceptance tests; whatever approach you take for this, the acceptance tests will generally be far longer running than the unit tests. For this reason, the acceptance tests should be undertaken out of the developer's workflow and run only after the build and unit tests have passed.

Once the acceptance tests have passed, you can deliver the system into the QA environment for further automated and manual testing in a representative environment. In this chapter, we will build the pipeline up until the deployment step, which is the subject of *Chapter 9, Storm on AWS*.

 There are many other test types that you should include in your pipeline. These include load and soak testing. It is important to understand the change in your system's performance over time.

How to do it...

1. Based on the previous recipes, you now have a working instance of Jenkins. Open it in your browser at `http://[IP]:8080`, and you should be presented with a blank Jenkins install, as shown in the following screenshot:

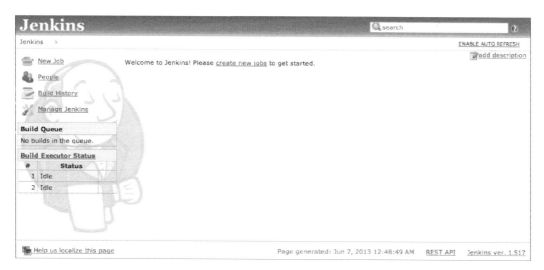

2. The first step is to install all the required plugins. Navigate to the **Manage Plugins** screen through the **Manage Jenkins** link in the main menu and install the following plugins. Then allow Jenkins to restart:

    ❑   Build Pipeline Plugin

    ❑   Git Plugin

    ❑   Dashboard View

3. Next, you must configure the first step in the build pipeline. Create a new Jenkins project called `rf-topology-build` and capture the following settings for the project:

    ❑   In **Source Code Management** (**Git**) change **Repository URL** to `https://bitbucket.org/qanderson/rf-topology.git` (or your URL) and **Branch** to `master`

    ❑   In **Build Triggers** change **Poll SCM** to `*/5 * * * *`

    ❑   In **Build** change **Root POM** to `pom.xml` and **Goals and options** to `clean package`

4. Save the project, and then kick off the first build by manually scheduling the build from the Jenkins home screen. You will then be presented with a progress bar:

5. By clicking on the progress bar, the actual console output of the build will be displayed.

How it works...

The CI simply polls the Git repo for changes, and when changes are detected, it kicks off a build using the goals specified in the project configuration. All artifacts and logs are then saved by the CI for later analysis. Jenkins will also keep track of the build progress for you over time:

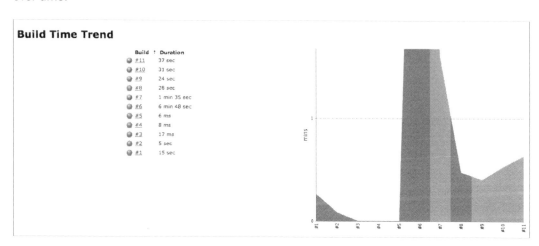

There's more...

If you have a private repository, you will need to configure the deployment keys for your repository. In order to achieve this, you need to generate an SSH key from the appropriate user on the CI server:

```
sudo su jenkins
ssh-keygen
```

Then, ensure that you have an SSH agent running and add your key:

```
ssh-agent /bin/bash
ssh-add ~/.ssh/id_rsa
```

You must then add your key to the repository; in order to get the key, just issue the following command, and then copy the output:

```
cat ~/.ssh/id_rsa.pub
```

If your repository is hosted on Bitbucket, you must use the following screen and paste the key:

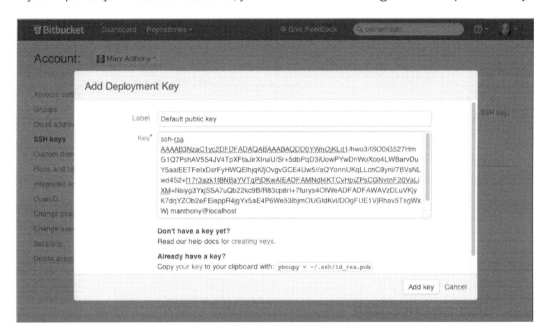

Once this is complete, you will need to update the URL for Git within your Jenkins project to use the SSH protocol. The new URL will be of the form `git@bitbucket.org:qanderson/rf-topology.git`.

Implementing automated acceptance testing

The automated acceptance test involves exercising a wide range of use cases across a wide range of test cases to achieve acceptable levels of test coverage at a system level. There are many technologies that can be used for such a process; however, often you need to implement quite complex logic, so using a traditional programming language and libraries is often a valid way to approach the problem. In this recipe, we will implement acceptance tests for the Random Forest topology and have them execute as part of the build pipeline.

Getting ready

You will be adding to your existing `rf-topology` implementation for this recipe; however, if you haven't completed the recipe from *Chapter 7, Real-time Machine Learning*, simply clone the instance from `https://bitbucket.org/qanderson/rf-topology.git`.

How to do it...

1. The acceptance test will be implemented as a unit test that only executes in a particular build phase. To start with, create a unit test in the `rf-topology` project. The first thing we need to do is define test data. The following is a sample of a single test case:

```
private static Map<String, Object[]> testData = new
HashMap<String, Object[]>();

    static {
        testData.put("d2e1e3d1", new Object[] {
                    "Hub2",
                    new double[] { 0.93, 0.84, 0.63, 0.79, 0.96,
                            0.71, 0.69, 0.68, 0.89, 0.77 } });
```

The test data essentially consists of an order ID, an expected output value (Hub2 in this case), and an array of inputs. Obviously, a single set of test data isn't valid for acceptance testing, so you must define a much larger set of test cases.

The test case will essentially undergo two phases: a warm-up phase and the actual test phase. The warm-up phase simply validates that everything is working correctly before injecting extra data into the scenario. Within each phase, we will send orders into the deployed topology, and then validate the outputs.

2. In order to send to a deployed topology, we must publish to the Kafka topic that will enable communications to that topology:

```
kafkaHost = System.getProperty("zk.host", "192.168.33.10");
        Properties props = new Properties();
        props.put("zk.connect", kafkaHost + ":" +
            Integer.toString(2181));
        props.put("serializer.class",
                    "kafka.serializer.StringEncoder");
        props.put("zk.connectiontimeout.ms", "1000000");
        props.put("groupid", "default_group");
        props.put("auto.commit", "true");
        ProducerConfig config = new ProducerConfig(props);
        producer = new Producer<String, String>(config);

        SimpleConsumer consumer = new
            SimpleConsumer(kafkaHost, 9092, 10000, 1024000);

        //warm up message
        double[] inputs = (double[])
            testData.values().iterator().next()[1];
        String input = createInput(inputs, "testOrder");
        ProducerData<String, String> data = new
            ProducerData<String, String>("orders", input);
        producer.send(data);
```

3. We then need to read from the output topic:

```
FetchRequest fetchRequest = new FetchRequest("order-output", 0,
offset, 1000000);
ByteBufferMessageSet messages =  consumer.fetch(fetchRequest);
            int warmUpAttempts = 0;
            boolean warm = false;
            while(!warm){
            Thread.sleep(2000);
                for (MessageAndOffset msg : messages) {
                    offset = msg.offset();
                    warm = true;
                }
                warmUpAttempts++;
                if(warmUpAttempts > 20)
                    fail("Too many tries trying to warm up");

            }
```

4. We then need to publish the complete test dataset:

```
for (String orderId : testData.keySet()) {
                    inputs = (double[]) testData.get(orderId)[1];
                    input = createInput(inputs, orderId);
                    data = new ProducerData<String,
                            String>("orders", input);
                    producer.send(data);

            }
```

5. We then need to read all the outputs and validate them:

```
int count = 0;
        int tested = 0;
        int errorCount = 0;
        while ((count < 10) && (tested < 100)) {
            fetchRequest = new FetchRequest("order-output", 0,
                                            offset, 1000000);
            messages = consumer.fetch(fetchRequest);
            for (MessageAndOffset msg : messages) {
                String test = new String(Utils.toByteArray
                            (msg.message().payload()));
                offset = msg.offset();
                JSONObject output = (JSONObject) JSONValue
                                        .parse(test);
                if (output != null) {
```

```
            String tempDispatchTo = (String)
                    output.get("dispatch-to");
            String tempOrderId = (String)
                    output.get("order-id");
            Object[] rhs = testData.get(tempOrderId);
            if (rhs != null) {
                String expected = (String) rhs[0];
                tested++;
                if (!expected.equals(tempDispatchTo))
                    errorCount++;
            }
        }
    }
    Thread.sleep(1000);
    count++;
}

assertEquals(100, tested);
assertTrue(errorCount < 3);
```

In order to validate the outputs, we need to remember that we won't get exact results from the predictive model, so we have to accept some level of error in the output.

6. The final change in the `rf-topology` project is to add the Maven configurations. We obviously don't want this long running test to execute with each build, so we need to configure the `surefire` plugin to exclude the test:

```
<plugin>
    <groupId>org.apache.maven.plugins</groupId>
    <artifactId>maven-surefire-plugin</artifactId>
    <version>2.14.1</version>
    <configuration>
        <excludes>
            <exclude>**/AcceptanceTest.java</exclude>
        </excludes>
    </configuration>
</plugin>
```

7. Then, configure the `failsafe` plugin to execute the test for us:

```
<plugin>
    <groupId>org.apache.maven.plugins</groupId>
    <artifactId>maven-failsafe-plugin</artifactId>
    <version>2.14.1</version>
    <configuration>
        <includes>
```

```
        <include>**/AcceptanceTest.java</include>
    </includes>
</configuration>
<executions>
    <execution>
        <id>integration-test</id>
        <goals>
            <goal>integration-test</goal>
        </goals>
    </execution>
</executions>
```

8. With the test in place, we need to add it to the build pipeline. Back in Jenkins, add a project to Jenkins called `rf-topology-local-acceptance`, with the following configuration properties:

    ❑   In **Source Code Management** (**Git**), change **Repository URL** to `https:// bitbucket.org/qanderson/rf-topology.git` (or your URL) and **Branch** to `master`

    ❑   In **Build Triggers**, set **Build after other projects are built** to `rf-topology-build`

    ❑   In **Pre Steps**, set **Command** to `cd /var/lib/jenkins/jobs/rf-topology-acceptance/workspace && /var/lib/jenkins/jobs/rf-topology-acceptance/workspace/pre-test.sh`

    ❑   In **Build**, set **Root POM** to `pom.xml` and **Goals and options** to `clean integration-test`

    ❑   In **Post Steps**, set **Command** to `pkill -9 -f storm.cookbook.OrderManagementTopology`

9. You can then save the project and manually schedule a build in order to test your configuration.

How it works...

The following diagram illustrates the process that is being undertaken within the context of the pipeline:

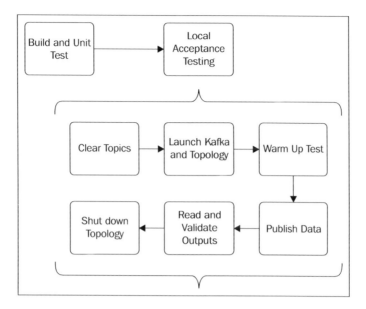

Details of each step is as follows:

- **Clear Topics**: It is important to have a clear set of topics, so that if you have failures, you have a single set of data to analyze. If there is other data existing in the topics, it will make analysis and debugging difficult.

- **Launch Kafka and the Topology**: Launch Kafka and the `rf-topology` in local mode. This is achieved through scripting and Maven goals.

- **Warm Up Test**: Perform the warm-up portion of the test.

- **Publish Data**: All the data is then published to the topic.

- **Read and Validate Outputs**: All the outputs are then read off the output topic and validated against the expected values.

- In order to perform these steps within Jenkins, we have a prestep and a poststep. In the prestep we specified the following command:

```
(cd /var/lib/jenkins/jobs/rf-topology-acceptance/workspace && /var/lib/
jenkins/jobs/rf-topology-acceptance/workspace/pre-test.sh)
```

The preceding command essentially ensures that a bash script is executed in the correct directory. The content of the script performs the tasks to clear the topics, to start up Kafka and the topology, using Maven:

```
#!/bin/sh

cwd=$(pwd)
KAFKA_HOME=/home/vagrant/kafka-0.7.2-incubating-src

#get a local build going
mvn clean package

#ensure we don't have any zookeeper, kafka or topology instances running
pkill -9 -f storm.cookbook.OrderManagementTopology
pkill -9 -f kafka
pkill -9 -f zookeeper
sleep 5

#remove all previous logs
rm -rfv /tmp/zookeeper
rm -rfv /tmp/kafka

#launch zookeeper and kafka
cd $KAFKA_HOME
bin/zookeeper-server-start.sh config/zookeeper.properties &
sleep 15
bin/kafka-server-start.sh config/server.properties &
sleep 5

cd $cwd
mvn exec:java -Dexec.classpathScope=compile -Dexec.mainClass=storm.
cookbook.OrderManagementTopology &
#allow some time for the topology to start
sleep 20
```

The tests are then executed via the integration-tests goal from Maven.

You can now create the pipeline view in order to see the pipeline in Jenkins. To do this, simply click on the **+** link on the main page and select **Build Pipeline View**. You will then have a view similar to the following on your main page under the **Views** tab:

This view is derived from the relationships between the Jenkins projects, specified by the "Triggered By" relationship between the projects.

There's more...

Obviously, generating all the test data manually isn't practical. There are two possible approaches to solve this problem. One would be to generate data and place it into a file that the test reads; the other would be to embed the data into the test. This is the approach listed previously. A Python script generated the code. The script is very similar to the one that was used to do functional testing in *Chapter 7, Real-time Machine Learning*, except that the line coercing generates Java code instead of CSV rows:

```
CUSTOMER_SEGMENTS = (
    [0.2, ["0", random.gauss, 0.25, 0.75, "%0.2f"]],
    [0.8, ["0", random.gauss, 1.5, 0.25, "%0.2f"]],
    [0.9, ["1", random.gauss, 0.6, 0.2, "%0.2f"]],
    [1.0, ["1", random.gauss, 0.75, 0.2, "%0.2f"]]
)


def gen_row (segments, num_col):
    coin_flip = random.random()

    for prob, rand_var in segments:
        if coin_flip <= prob:
            (label, dist, mean, sigma, format) = rand_var
            order_id = str(uuid.uuid1()).split("-")[0]
            return map(lambda x: format % dist(mean, sigma),
                    range(0, num_col)) + [label]
```

```python
def print_row (segments, num_col):
    stdout.write("testData.put (\"")
    order_id = str(uuid.uuid1()).split("-")[0]
    stdout.write( order_id )
    stdout.write( "\", new Object[]{" )
    values =  gen_row(segments, num_col)
    if values[len(values)-1] == "0":
        stdout.write( "\"Hub1\"" )
    else:
        stdout.write( "\"Hub2\"" )
    stdout.write( ", new double[] { " )
    for x in range(0, len(values)-1):
        stdout.write( str(values[x]) )
        if x < (len(values)-2):
            stdout.write( "," )
    stdout.write( "}});\n" )


if __name__ == '__main__':
    for i in range(0, 100):
        print_row(CUSTOMER_SEGMENTS, 10)
```

This script has been tested using Python 2.7; simply execute it and use the output as the test data within your test case.

9
Storm on AWS

In this chapter we will cover:

- ▶ Deploying Storm on AWS using Pallet
- ▶ Setting up a Virtual Private Cloud
- ▶ Deploying Storm into Virtual Private Cloud using Vagrant

Introduction

Software is ultimately an academic exercise unless it adds value in a production environment. In this chapter, we will explore how to deliver Storm solutions into the **Amazon Web Services' Elastic Compute Cloud** (**AWS EC2**). This isn't the only cloud hosting provider you might want to use, there are many good **Platform as a Service** (**PaaS**) providers, and many of them are excellent and also have high levels of automation and availability. The choice of AWS for the book is simply because it is extremely cheap and easy to get started, which is ideal for learning, but it also allows you to go from the basic deployments all the way through to complete **Virtual Private Cloud** (**VPC**), complete with multiple isolated subnets, firewalls, and appropriate IPSEC. These are all important concepts in an enterprise delivery, which you can learn quickly using AWS EC2 and VPC as presented in this chapter; however, the concepts and the tools are by no means tied to AWS.

You will learn to deploy Storm using the community-recommended method of **Pallet Ops**, which is a Clojure-based cloud infrastructure automation framework. You will also learn to extend your original development environment scripts from *Chapter 1, Setting Up Your Development Environment*, all the way through to production, based on Vagrant and Puppet provisioning. None of these frameworks are tied in any way to AWS. Pallet is designed to work with any cloud provider supported by jclouds, which are over 20 at the time of writing this book and counting. Vagrant supports multiple providers from Version 1.1 onwards. It currently supports VirtualBox, AWS, and VMware, with new providers being released from the community each day.

The point therefore, is to learn the tools and concepts that will equip you to deploy Storm effectively and securely into any production environment you are faced with. As an added bonus, you will get an introduction to build a secure production environment from scratch, on AWS, which you may simply choose to use for your particular implementation.

Deploying Storm on AWS using Pallet

The Storm deploy module is recommended by the community for the deployment of Storm clusters on AWS. It is available at `https://github.com/nathanmarz/storm-deploy`, and like Storm itself, was built by *Nathan Marz*. And like the Storm project, it has really excellent documentation. Because of this fact, this recipe is heavily based on the content of that wiki.

Storm deploy is based on Pallet. Pallet is a node provisioning, configuration and administration tool written in Clojure. It is designed to simplify small to midsize deployments. At this stage, it is useful to quickly introduce and position Pallet quickly within the context of infrastructure deployments, Storm, and the other chapters of this book.

Pallet has the following few properties that are worth mentioning:

- It has no inherent dependencies that must be installed on the nodes being managed. This makes it highly portable, supporting just about any image out there.

- Pallet has no central server. It can simply be run whenever required from anywhere.

- Everything is in version control.

These properties are quite important. The provisioning, presented in *Chapter 1, Setting Up Your Development Environment*, exhibits similar qualities. At this point, it is therefore useful to ask and answer the question: Why present two competing provisioning frameworks? The following elements answer this question:

- Pallet is the community-recommended method for deployment to AWS.

- Vagrant originally provided portable development environments only. However, it has matured into a technology that can be leveraged throughout the delivery process and lifecycle. It is therefore extremely attractive, especially if one intends to implement DevOps or continuous delivery to some extent. Vagrant allows the deployment process to be established early in your development environments, and then to be repeatedly verified through various environments with little or no change. It must be noted that this is possible with Pallet too, but Vagrant is far more simple to use.

- Many organizations have standardized on particular technologies, one of the reasons being to leverage the skills and training spend. In the DevOps communities, Puppet and Chef are more widely used than Pallet. Moreover, your organization may already have a collection of recipes or modules they would prefer to extend instead of introducing another technology within the operations space, given that variables in that space are not a good thing.

- In keeping with the theme of the book, various approaches are presented for a given problem in the hope that this will not only reach a wider audience, but also help to reinforce the understanding of the underlying concepts.

In *Chapter 1, Setting Up Your Development Environment*, you were introduced to the concept of provisioning concerns in three distinct layers. I will present the concept here again for convenience of being able to contrast the positioning of Pallet and Vagrant/Puppet:

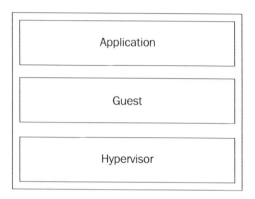

In the interests of clarity, Vagrant provides the functionality to provision at the hypervisor layer and enables the Guest and Application provisioning through Puppet, Chef, and shell scripts. Pallet, on the other hand, covers all three layers.

Over and above these differences, Pallet and the recipes presented here and in *Chapter 1, Setting Up Your Development Environment*, attempt to achieve the following things:

- Automate as far as possible
- Minimize or remove guest dependencies to maximize image coverage
- Implement distributed provisioning
- Keep everything in version control

Getting ready

In order to proceed with this recipe, you need a valid **AWS** account. Perform the following steps:

1. Navigate to `http://aws.amazon.com/` in your browser.
2. Click on the **Sign Up** button, which will take you to the sign-in page.
3. Select the **I am a new user** option and enter your e-mail address.
4. Complete the account form.
5. Complete your payment information.
6. Complete the registration process by entering your identification verification information.

Once you have signed up, you need to create a set of credentials to be used:

1. Navigate to `https://console.aws.amazon.com` in your browser.

2. Log in and then select **IAM** from the main menu.

3. Select users from the menu bar to the left.

4. Click on the **Create new user** button at the top of the page.

5. Enter a username and click on **Create**.

6. You will then be presented with a dialog box, as shown in the following screenshot:

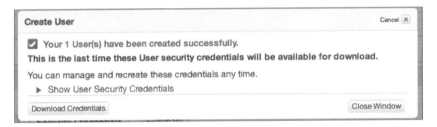

Ensure that you download the credentials at this point and place them somewhere safe. You won't get another opportunity to download them.

How to do it...

1. Start by cloning the `storm-deploy` project and resolving the dependencies on your local machine:

    ```
    git clone https://github.com/nathanmarz/storm-deploy.git
    cd storm-deploy
    lein deps
    ```

2. Create a file named `config.clj` under `~/.pallet/` with the following content, specialized for your case:

    ```
    (defpallet
      :services
      {
        :default {
                  :blobstore-provider "aws-s3"
                  :provider "aws-ec2"
                  :environment {:user {:username "storm"   ; this must
                                        be "storm"
                                       :private-key-path "$YOUR_
                                       PRIVATE_KEY_PATH$"
    ```

```
                                      :public-key-path "$YOUR_PUBLIC_
                                      KEY_PATH$"}
                          :aws-user-id "$YOUR_USER_ID$"}
                :identity "$YOUR_AWS_ACCESS_KEY$"
                :credential "$YOUR_AWS_ACCESS_KEY_SECRET$"
                :jclouds.regions "$YOUR_AWS_REGION$"
                }
        })
```

The details of each field are as follows:

- `private-key-path`: Your private key path. If you don't have a private key yet, you can generate it using the `:ssh-keygen` command. This will generate a private and public key at `~/.ssh/id_rsa`.

- `public-key-path`: This is the path to your private key, which should be : `~/.ssh/id_rsa.pub`.

- `aws-user-id`: You can find this on your account management page. It's a numeric number with hyphens in it.

- `identity`: Your AWS access key contained in your user creation download.

- `credential`: Your AWS access key secret contained in your user creation download.

- `jclouds.regions`: The region that you will be using for the deployment. For example, : `us-east-1`.

 For more information on getting started with AWS, please visit their documentation at `http://docs.aws.amazon.com/AWSEC2/latest/UserGuide/EC2_GetStarted.html`.

3. Next, you must configure your cluster properties. You can do this by editing `conf/clusters.yaml`. You can change the number of zookeeper nodes or supervisor nodes by editing `zookeeper.count` or `supervisor.count`, respectively. You can launch spot instances for supervisor nodes by setting a value for `supervisor.spot.price`.

4. Once these configurations are in place, you can simply run the following command in order to launch your cluster:

```
lein deploy-storm --start --name mycluster --release {release
version}
```

The `--name` parameter names your cluster so that you can attach to it or stop it later. If you omit `--name`, it will default to `dev`. The `--release` parameter indicates which release of Storm to install. If you omit `--release`, it will install Storm from the master branch. You should rather specify a specific stable release.

The `deploy` sets up Zookeeper, sets up Nimbus, launches the Storm UI on port 8080 on Nimbus, launches a DRPC server on port 3772 on Nimbus, sets up the Supervisors, sets configurations appropriately, sets the appropriate permissions for the security groups, and attaches your machine to the cluster.

Running this `deploy` will create multiple EC2 nodes on AWS. As a result, AWS will start charging your account for the time that these nodes execute. Make sure that you have estimated and understood the costs involved before you get an unexpected bill.

There's more...

Storm `deploy` automatically attaches your machine to the cluster so that you can manage it through the `start` and `stop` commands for the cluster. Attaching to a cluster configures your Storm client to talk to that particular cluster as well as authorizes your computer to view the Storm UI.

To attach to a cluster, run the following command:

```
lein deploy-storm --attach --name mycluster
```

Attaching does the following:

▶ Writes the location of Nimbus in `~/.storm/storm.yaml` so that the Storm client knows which cluster to talk to

▶ Authorizes your computer to access the Nimbus daemon's Thrift port (which is used for submitting topologies)

▶ Authorizes your computer to access the Storm UI on port 8080 on Nimbus

▶ Authorizes your computer to access Ganglia on port 80 on Nimbus

Note that these instructions can be found on the Storm deploy wiki (`https://github.com/nathanmarz/storm-deploy`), and are placed here for your convenience.

The Storm deploy installs both the Storm UI and Ganglia. **Ganglia** is a scalable distributed monitoring system for high-performance computing systems, such as clusters and grids. In order to get the IPs for your cluster, simply execute the following command:

```
lein deploy-storm --ips --name mycluster
```

Setting up a Virtual Private Cloud

According to Amazon, a Virtual Private Cloud is defined as follows:

> *Amazon Virtual Private Cloud (Amazon VPC) lets you provision a logically isolated section of the Amazon Web Services (AWS) Cloud where you can launch AWS resources in a virtual network that you define. You have complete control over your virtual networking environment, including selection of your own IP address range, creation of subnets, and configuration of route tables and network gateways.*

This is an exceptionally powerful feature of the **AWS** cloud service offering. It essentially allows you to set up an enterprise strength set of environments, from development through to production, which are secure, isolated, and securely connected to your own internal networks. Network-level isolation is essential for the long-term security of a production system.

A typical enterprise solution will comprise of multiple layers of network, each with varying levels of access, representing layers of added security in order to protect the most vital portions of a system. There are many possible reference architectures, each appropriate for a given solution. In order to illustrate the nature of the isolated networks within the context of an enterprise solution, we need to have a solution that consists of a traditional web application, which feeds events through to the Storm cluster asynchronously for processing.

A potential deployment architecture could be as follows:

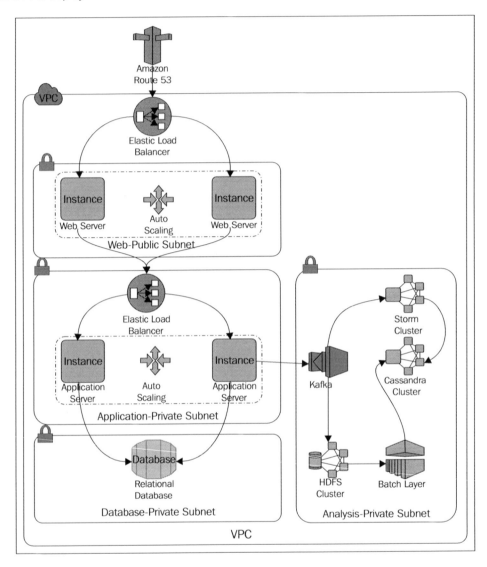

What you will notice in this picture is that the various functions of the solution are isolated at the Network level. A public-facing subnet makes the web servers available via load balancing and Elastic IP addresses. The application servers are isolated into their own subnet, with appropriate firewall rules, ensuring that the inward connections are only from specified IPs and ports within the web subnet. These connections are also only established through appropriate cryptographic relationships between the Web and application servers. This ensures that no services are incorrectly exposed from the application server.

Moving down the stack, a similar approach is applied to the database, which is typically a cluster too.

Asynchronous events are published from the application server to the analysis stack, via messaging, in this case **Kafka**. These events are then consumed and processed by Storm and are saved into HDFS as immutable events, directly from Kafka or from Storm itself, depending on the structure of the topology.

The exact layout of the networks is not the purpose of this recipe or chapter. One always needs to define an appropriate functional, conceptual, and deployment architecture for their given set of requirements. The purpose of this recipe is to show how to set up a VPC with a public and private subnet. In the next chapter, you will learn to deploy a Storm cluster into the private subnet. Using this experience, you will then be equipped to design and implement a deployment architecture as complex as the one illustrated previously. This will ensure that you can position Storm as a key element within your production environments, even in environments where regulatory constraints exist.

The environment that we will create in the next two recipes is best described by the following diagram:

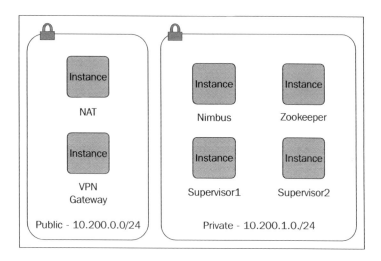

How to do it...

1. You will implement this recipe using the AWS console, so to start, log in to the console and select **VPC** from the dropdown of services. You should be presented with a screen similar to the following:

2. Start by clicking on the **Start VPC Wizard** button and selecting the **VPC with Public and Private Subnets** option. This will create two subnets for you, together with a preconfigured EC2-based NAT instance. The NAT instance will allow your nodes within the private subnet to access the Internet.

 Nodes that aren't associated with an Elastic IP won't be able to access the Internet without a well-configured NAT instance in place.

3. Next, you will be presented with a screen similar to the following, which allows you to specify the network IP CIDR blocks and other settings for your VPC:

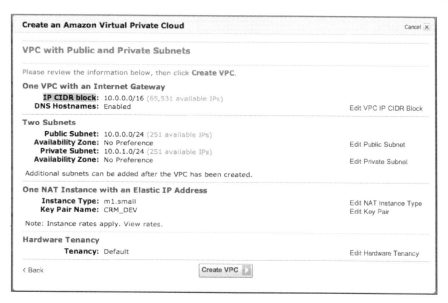

4. At this point, you need to carefully choose your IP addresses. You will also need to specify the key pair that will gain you access to administer your NAT instance.

While the defaults are good values, you must be careful not to use the same blocks as the local network. If you will use the same IP blocks, you are likely to experience route configuration issues and conflicts. These sorts of issues are notoriously difficult to debug, so rather avoid them.

5. Update the IP blocks such that the public subnet is `10.200.0.0/24` and the private subnet is `10.200.1.0/24`, and then create the VPC.

Congratulations, you have created your first AWS VPC with a pubic and private subnet. You can now review the subnets and the NAT instance that has been created. You can verify the NAT instance by identifying it in the EC2 instance list and connecting to it:

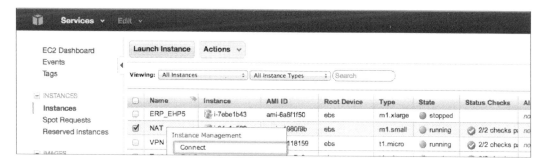

In order to access and provision into the private network, we need to set up an IPSEC-based VPN access to the private network. We do this because we don't want to allocate Elastic IPs to our Storm nodes; there is no good reason for anyone on the Internet to have the ability to connect to our Storm nodes.

6. We will use OpenVPN for this purpose. From within the EC2 instance list screen, click on the **Launch Instance** button, select the classic wizard, and then enter **OpenVPN Access Server** under the **Community AMIs** tab. Select the displayed AMI and create the instance, ensuring that it is added to the public subnet that you have just created (`10.200.0.0/24`). As part of the creation of the instance, create a new security group and open the following ports:

   ❏ TCP, 22 from 0.0.0.0/0

   ❏ TCP, 443 from 0.0.0.0/0

   ❏ TCP, 943 from 0.0.0.0/0

   ❏ UDP, 1194 from 0.0.0.0/0

 Always assign good descriptive names to your instances after creation; this will make your life much easier in future steps.

7. Next, you need to provide an Elastic IP to the OpenVPN instance. Select **Elastic IPs** from the menu on the left-hand side, and then allocate a new address. Once it is allocated, associate it with the newly created OpenVPN instance. Take note of the IP address, because you will need it soon.

8. Next, verify your security group and change the source/destination check on the node. Your security group settings should look like the following:

9. And you can disable the source/destination check for the instance from the instance context menu:

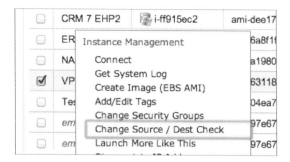

10. Next, you need to set up the OpenVPN software on the instance. Connect to the instance using SSH. The exact command can be found from the context menu under **Connect**.

    When connected for the first time, the console will prompt you for setup answers for OpenVPN. Accept all the default values, except the user credential store, which you should not make local unless you have another means of authentication available.

11. Once the setup process is complete, you will be presented with a standard bash console as the root user. You must now assign a password to the OpenVPN user:

    `passwd openvpn`

12. Once this is complete, you can exit the console and open the following link in your browser: `https://[ElasticIP]:943/admin/`.

13. Log in with the user `openvpn` and the password that you just chose. Once you have accepted the terms and conditions, navigate to the **Server Network Settings**:

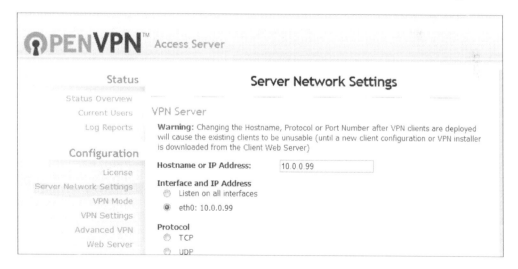

14. Change the value of **Hostname or IP address** to the Elastic IP address for this instance:

15. Ensure that you save the settings, select the VPN settings, and add both subnets to the routing section:

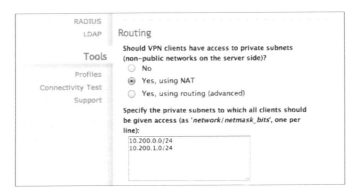

16. Ensure that you save the settings and then select the button to update the running server:

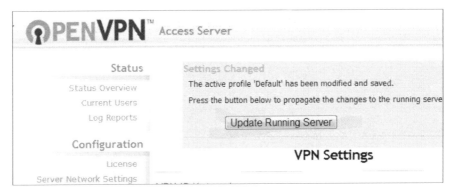

You now have a functioning VPN server. Next, you need to install the client and connect. But before you do that, we need to test the access to the private subnet. In order to do this, we need an instance in the subnet.

17. Create a micro test node in that subnet using a standard Ubuntu image from the EC2 instance list using the wizard. Ensure that you don't assign it an Elastic IP, and try to connect to the instance via SSH from your machine. It should fail.

18. We can now make the VPN client connection and test again. To do this, navigate in your browser to the VPN server client interface at `https://[ElasticIP]:943/`. Log in using the `openvpn` user and follow the onscreen prompts to download the client software and connect.

19. You should now be able to connect to the private IP of the testing node via SSH from your local machine. Finally, you need to validate that the testing node has Internet access. You can do this simply by performing a ping operation:

```
ping www.google.com
```

Deploying Storm into Virtual Private Cloud using Vagrant

In *Chapter 1, Setting Up Your Development Environment*, we explored portal development using Vagrant; we even deployed a full Storm cluster into a local set of virtual machines. This gave us a realistic way of testing the deployment and interactions of a cluster. It is however very limited, in that all virtual machines are hosted on your local developer system.

In IT operations, it is important to reduce the number of variables and the number of things that need to be changed or configured in a system in order to promote it through different environments. For that reason, it is wise to standardize an operating system's databases and tool chains across environments, and have the developer's environments mimic all the other environments as closely as possible. Vagrant provides an excellent way of achieving this. Using Vagrant, you can develop a complete environment on your local machine, as we learned in *Chapter 1, Setting Up Your Development Environment*, and then use the same scripts to promote the deployment into the next environment, provided it is based on a supported Vagrant provider. This is an extremely powerful workflow process for a development team. It enables developers to automate deployments and test them repeatedly throughout the development process, thus greatly reducing the effort and risk of promoting the code through test and into production.

In this final recipe, we will learn how to add the **AWS** provider configuration to our cluster deployment scripts from *Chapter 1, Setting Up Your Development Environment*, and then deploy a full Storm cluster into the private subnet we created in the previous recipe.

Getting ready

Before you begin this recipe, ensure that you have a valid key pair that you can use for the deployment process. Ensure that you have the name handy and know the path of the .pem file that you downloaded previously. If you don't have a key pair, simply select **Key Pairs** from the EC2 services area in the AWS console, and then click on **Create Key Pair**.

How to do it...

1. To start with, we need to install the Vagrant AWS provider plugin and add the required Vagrant box. We do this simply from the command line using the following command:

```
vagrant plugin install vagrant-aws
```

```
vagrant box add dummy https://github.com/mitchellh/vagrant-aws/
raw/master/dummy.box
```

2. Next, we need to add the AWS settings to the Vagrant file for our cluster. Edit the Vagrant file within your `vagrant-storm-cluster` project from the first chapter. There are numerous changes that we need to make to the file, so let's go through them one by one. Right at the top of the file, we specified all the properties for each machine in the virtual cluster. We need to update this to include some properties we need for AWS, essentially adding the instance type:

```
boxes = [
    { :name => :nimbus, :ip => '10.200.1.100', :cpus =>2, :memory =>
      512, :instance => 'm1.small' },
    { :name => :supervisor1, :ip => '10.200.1.101', :cpus =>4,
      :memory => 1024, :instance => 'm1.medium' },
    { :name => :supervisor2, :ip => '10.200.1.102', :cpus =>4,
      :memory => 1024, :instance => 'm1.medium' },
    { :name => :zookeeper1, :ip => '10.200.1.201', :cpus =>1,
      :memory => 1024, :instance => 'm1.small' },
]
```

3. Next, we need to define the region and AMI that we are going to use (remember to replace the region as appropriate, together with the related AMI):

```
AWS_REGION = ENV['AWS_REGION'] || "ap-southeast-2"
AWS_AMI    = ENV['AWS_AMI']    || "ami-97e675ad"
```

The AMI was chosen out of a list of standard Ubuntu AMIs from the Ubuntu AMI Locator at http://cloud-images.ubuntu.com/locator/ec2/.

4. Next, we need to add the AWS configurations required:

```
config.vm.provider :aws do |aws, override|
        config.vm.box = "dummy"
          aws.access_key_id = "identity"
          aws.secret_access_key = "credential"
          aws.keypair_name = "KeyPairName"
          aws.region = AWS_REGION
          aws.ami    = AWS_AMI
          aws.private_ip_address = opts[:ip]
          aws.subnet_id = "subnet-xxxx"
          override.ssh.username = "ubuntu"
          override.ssh.private_key_path = xxx.pem"
          aws.instance_type = opts[:instance]
        end
config.vm.provision :shell, :inline => "hostname storm.%s" %
opts[:name].to_s
```

Replace the following values with the appropriate values for your situation:

- ❏ `identity`: Your AWS access key, contained in your user creation download.

- ❏ `credential`: Your AWS access key secret, contained in your user creation download.

- ❏ `KeyPairName`: The name of the key pair that you will use in the deployments.

- ❏ `subnet-xxxx`: The ID of the private subnet. This can be obtained from the VPC console, under **Subnets**. Ensure that this is the ID of the private subnet.

- ❏ `xxx.pem`: The fully-qualified path to the `.pem` file of the key pair generated by AWS previously. This file must correspond to the key pair name provided previously.

5. Finally, there is a fundamental difference between VirtualBox boxes and Vagrant boxes for the AWS provider. In the case of the AWS provider, we will use an actual AMI, which is not necessarily geared for Vagrant. In the case of the previous AMI, it isn't; it is a vanilla Ubuntu AMI. In the case of the VirtualBox images, they are built with Vagrant in mind, which means that they have certain dependencies already in place. In this case, the only dependency that the AMI is missing is the installation of Puppet, which we need for the provisioning. This can be rectified through a simple command-line provisioning step:

```
config.vm.provision :shell, :inline => "apt-get --yes --force-yes
install puppet"
```

6. With all these additions to the Vagrant file, we can simply update the Vagrant up command slightly in order to provision the cluster onto AWS:

```
vagrant up --provider=aws
```

 Once this command has completed successfully, you can simply issue Vagrant commands as you normally would. As an optimization, you could choose to move the data files into an S3 bucket, instead of having them synchronized from the local data folder.

7. Note that this is only slightly different from the local deployment:

```
vagrant up
```

Once the provisioning is complete, you will have a complete Storm cluster, which is accessible only within the private subnet via VPN.

Index

Thank you for buying
Storm Real-time Processing Cookbook

About Packt Publishing

Packt, pronounced 'packed', published its first book "*Mastering phpMyAdmin for Effective MySQL Management*" in April 2004 and subsequently continued to specialize in publishing highly focused books on specific technologies and solutions.

Our books and publications share the experiences of your fellow IT professionals in adapting and customizing today's systems, applications, and frameworks. Our solution based books give you the knowledge and power to customize the software and technologies you're using to get the job done. Packt books are more specific and less general than the IT books you have seen in the past. Our unique business model allows us to bring you more focused information, giving you more of what you need to know, and less of what you don't.

Packt is a modern, yet unique publishing company, which focuses on producing quality, cutting-edge books for communities of developers, administrators, and newbies alike. For more information, please visit our website: www.packtpub.com.

About Packt Open Source

In 2010, Packt launched two new brands, Packt Open Source and Packt Enterprise, in order to continue its focus on specialization. This book is part of the Packt Open Source brand, home to books published on software built around Open Source licences, and offering information to anybody from advanced developers to budding web designers. The Open Source brand also runs Packt's Open Source Royalty Scheme, by which Packt gives a royalty to each Open Source project about whose software a book is sold.

Writing for Packt

We welcome all inquiries from people who are interested in authoring. Book proposals should be sent to author@packtpub.com. If your book idea is still at an early stage and you would like to discuss it first before writing a formal book proposal, contact us; one of our commissioning editors will get in touch with you.

We're not just looking for published authors; if you have strong technical skills but no writing experience, our experienced editors can help you develop a writing career, or simply get some additional reward for your expertise.

SignalR: Real-time Application Development

ISBN: 978-1-78216-424-1   Paperback: 124 pages

Utilize real-time functionality in your .Net applications with ease

1. Develop real-time applications across numerous platforms

2. Create scalable applications that are ready for cloud deployment

3. Utilize the full potential of SignalR

Instant PhpStorm Starter

ISBN: 978-1-84969-394-3   Paperback: 86 pages

Learn professional PHP development with PhpStorm

1. Learn something new in an Instant! A short, fast, focused guide delivering immediate results.

2. Learn PHPStorm from scratch, from downloading to installation with no prior knowledge required

3. Enter, modify, and inspect the source code with as much automation as possible

4. Simple, full of easy-to-follow procedures and intuitive illustrations, this book will set you speedily on the right track

Please check **www.packtpub.com** for information on our titles

Real-time Web Application Development with Vert.x

ISBN: 978-1-78216-795-2   Paperback: 117 pages

An intuitive guide to building applications for the real-time web with the vert.x platform

1. Get started with developing applications for the real-time web

2. From concept to deployment, learn the full development workflow of a real-time web application

3. Utilize the Java skills you already have while stepping up to the next level

Socket.IO Real-time Web Application Development

ISBN: 978-1-78216-078-6   Paperback: 140 pages

Build modern real-time web applications powered by Socket.IO

1. Understand the usage of various socket.io features like rooms, namespaces, and sessions

2. Secure the socket.io communication

3. Deploy and scale your socket.io and Node.js applications in production

4. A practical guide that quickly gets you up and running with socket.io

Please check **www.packtpub.com** for information on our titles

31800614R10144

Made in the USA
Lexington, KY
28 April 2014